101 Questions and Answers
On Demon Powers

by
Dr. Lester Sumrall

HARRISON HOUSE
Tulsa, Oklahoma

Unless otherwise indicated,
all Scripture quotations are taken from
the *King James Version* of the Bible.

3rd Printing
Over 30,000 in Print

101 Questions and Answers On Demon Powers
ISBN 0-89274-261-5
Copyright © 1983 by Lester Sumrall Evangelistic
   Association, Inc.
P. O. Box 12
South Bend, Indiana 46624

Published by Harrison House, Inc.
P. O. Box 35035
Tulsa, Oklahoma 74153

Preface

In my travels in over one hundred nations of the world, I have been repeatedly asked questions regarding eschatology (the doctrine of the last or final things). Often it is a direct question regarding the reality and the functioning of satanic and demon powers. In many instances I have found that the inquiring persons needed answers to some unusual phenomena which had occurred in their community or home.

I find it quite baffling that people in what we term "heathen lands" know more about the negative forces of evil than many church people living in our Western civilization.

Personally, I feel it is time for Christians to become acquainted with the unseen world of the spirit, both negative and positive. Much of our modern civilization is too materialistically minded. However, some scientists are coming to realize that there is a real world of the spirit, and they are delving into its mysteries at this present time. Also, multitudes of inquiring people are dabbling in spiritism and other non-biblical cults.

To counterbalance this activity, today's Christian must possess the positive power of God and be a living witness to the Spirit of God. The Apostle Paul was very strong to say that *we are not ignorant of his* (Satan's) *devices* (2 Cor. 2:11). You and I must not be ignorant of them either. The Lord Jesus wants His Church to set multitudes free. He said, *If the Son therefore shall make you free, ye shall be free indeed* (John 8:36).

The purpose of this book is to reveal the true potential of the followers of Christ to set individuals, communities, or nations free from any evil force of the enemy. There has never been a time when people were so eager for the right answers. This is especially true in the realm of the unseen spirit world.

— Lester Sumrall

101 Questions and Answers On Demon Powers

1. Does anyone know the origin of the devil?

Yes, the Bible is very careful to explain the origin of the devil because all evil comes from him. God has recorded more than 200 biblical references to a personal force of evil known as the devil.

His evilness began long before the Garden of Eden, and his wickedness has continued throughout each succeeding dispensation. His evilness will be cut short just before the Millennium, or thousand-year reign of Christ, after which he will be released again for a short season. (Rev. 20:1-3.)

The devil is known to those who study the Bible as the key to all human tragedy, ill-will, and hatred. To understand our present world situations, it is necessary to turn the divine spotlight on the devil.

God relates to us in Isaiah 14:12-15:

How art thou fallen from heaven, O Lucifer, son of the morning! how art thou cut down to the ground, which didst weaken the nations!

For thou hast said in thine heart, I will ascend into heaven, I will exalt my throne above the stars of God: I will sit also upon the mount of the congregation, in the sides of the north:

I will ascend above the heights of the clouds; I will be like the most High.

Yet thou shalt be brought down to hell, to the sides of the pit.

Further, God reveals the origin of the devil in Ezekiel 28:13-17:

Thou hast been in Eden the garden of God; every precious stone was thy covering . . .

Thou art the anointed cherub that covereth; and I have set thee so: thou wast upon the holy mountain of God; thou hast walked up and down in the midst of the stones of fire.

Thou wast perfect in thy ways from the day that thou wast created, till iniquity was found in thee.

By the multitude of thy merchandise they have filled the midst of thee with violence, and thou hast sinned: therefore I will cast thee as profane out of the mountain of God: and I will destroy thee, O covering cherub, from the midst of the stones of fire.

Thine heart was lifted up because of thy beauty, thou hast corrupted thy wisdom by reason of thy brightness: I will cast thee to the ground, I will lay thee before kings, that they may behold thee.

The devil was created an archangel. He possessed perfection of beauty and wisdom. He was named "son of the morning." No other creature was given such a name. He was called "the anointed cherub" and was elevated to a special and privileged place. His very garments were made of precious stones, reflecting the blazing glory of the Trinity.

How did this glorious archangel become the devil? The Bible is very careful to tell us: *Thine heart was lifted up because of thy beauty, thou hast corrupted thy wisdom by reason of thy brightness* (Ezek. 28:17). This means that pride came into his heart. By looking upon himself rather than upon the Most High, Lucifer decided that his greatness and beauty came from within himself.

In Isaiah 14:13,14 he said ''I will'' five times, thus revealing the pride in his heart. He caused rebellion in heaven, possibly causing one third of the angelic host to become subordinated to him to battle the Almighty. He caused those angelic spirits to be removed from heaven. *And his tail drew the third part of the stars of heaven, and did cast them to the earth* (Rev. 12:4).

Therefore, God did **not** make the devil. Lucifer, the archangel, made himself the devil. Then he was expelled from heaven and demoted to his present position.

In Ezekiel 28:15 God said to Lucifer, *Thou wast perfect in thy ways from the day that thou wast created, till iniquity was found in thee.*

Yes, the Bible does give the origin of the devil. It gives his known action in heaven from whence he was expelled. The Bible related his wicked deceptions in the Garden of Eden, where he caused man to fall from God's favor, marking the beginning of a titantic struggle between good and evil.

The devil's last action will be at the Battle of Gog and Magog, before being forever confined and tormented in the Lake of Fire. (Rev. 20:7-10.)

2. Isn't the devil just an impersonal influence?

If that question is meant to imply that a personality called the devil does not actually exist, I must disagree. Satan does possess a sinister influence, but he is very much a real person. Over 200 times in the Bible direct reference is made to his personality. The name *Satan* is used 54 times. In Matthew 4:10 Jesus says, *Get thee hence, Satan.*

The Apostle Paul tells us in 2 Corinthians 11:14, *Satan himself is transformed into an angel of light.* This describes a personality.

The Apostle Peter, revealing the great anger and strength of the devil, declares him to be *as a roaring lion* (1 Pet. 5:8). This description certainly represents a personality.

John refers to the devil as *the dragon* (Rev. 20:2), describing his awful destruction upon humanity.

Jesus said of the devil in John 8:44: *He . . . abode not in the truth.* It takes a personality to depart from the truth.

The devil is also called:

that Wicked (2 Thess. 2:8).

the god of this world (2 Cor. 4:4).

the tempter (1 Thess. 3:5).

the power of darkness (Col. 1:13).

your adversary (1 Pet. 5:8).

the accuser of our brethren (Rev. 12:10).

the prince of the devils (Matt. 12:24).

In James 4:7, we are told to *resist the devil, and he will flee . . . .*

These scriptures prove that there is indeed an evil personality who seeks to destroy all that God has made in this universe.

3. Is God pleased with discussions about the devil?

The entire Bible must be discussed. The positive truth is so good when we know the negative side as well. We must know the designs of our enemy, or we will be unable to successfully combat him.

If God is not pleased with our discussing the forces of evil, why did Jesus say more about evil than He did about any other subject in the Bible?

The only one I know who does not want the devil discussed is the devil himself. His reasons for seeking anonymity are the same reasons the Mafia and the underground syndicates seek to avoid public scrutiny. Leaders of organized crime don't want to be revealed for what they are. Neither does Satan.

If this question refers to constant talking about the devil, I would say that I personally spend more than ninety percent of my time preaching about the greatness of Christ and the blessings of Christian living. I think on those things which are spiritually edifying. When it is necessary to reveal the evil of our times, I certainly believe that God is pleased when we do so.

4. Is it dangerous to talk about the devil?

I cannot see where discussing our enemy has any wrong or any danger associated with it.

The Lord Jesus told us more about the devil than any other person in the entire Bible. He renounced and denounced the devil more than any other person of which we have record. He gave strict orders to His apostles to cast out devils. (Luke 9:1; Matt. 10:1.) The seventy disciples sent out by Jesus returned, rejoicing that they had power over devils. (Luke 10:17.) In the Great Commission, our Lord stated: *And these signs shall follow them that believe; In my name shall they cast out devils* (Mark 16:17).

It appears that the less we say about the devil, the greater gains he makes in the world. Possibly he would like to silence those who would destroy him and his works.

There are people who, if you speak about the devil, accuse you of being negative. However, I am sure that this is all part of the devil's strategy to keep people quiet about him. People in ignorance easily fall prey to the wiles of the devil. Enlightened people know how to stay free from his powers.

In the darkened heathen lands, he walks forth boldly to bind and destroy, and no one is able to stand up against him. In Christian lands we can say like Paul, *We are not ignorant of his devices* (2 Cor. 2:11).

Satan quickly recognizes those who are able to control him. He spoke to the seven sons of Sceva and said, *Jesus I know, and Paul I know; but who are ye?* (Acts 19:15).

I personally feel that it is not a **discussion** which is needed with the devil, but a **confrontation.** Jesus Christ came to destroy the works of Satan (1 John 3:8), and we are in the same business. Every day we should learn better how to destroy him. We do not discuss him in fear, but we speak of him in the light of the great victory achieved over him by the Lord Jesus Christ through His death and resurrection. We stand sheltered in the blood of Jesus Christ against every power of the devil. Christ promised His disciples: *Behold, I give unto you power to tread on serpents and scorpions, and over all the power of the enemy: and nothing shall by any means hurt you* (Luke 10:19). We believe this and live by it.

5. What is the origin of demons?

One must remember that there is one devil, but many demons. The devil is prince of demons. (Matt. 12:24.) Demons, as described in the Bible, are the angelic host who decided to follow Lucifer, the archangel, in his insurrection against God. Luke 10:18 says, *And he* (Jesus) *said unto them, I beheld Satan as lightning fall from heaven.*

Revelation 12:3,4,7-9 tells us:

And there appeared another wonder in heaven; and behold a great red dragon, having seven heads and ten horns, and seven crowns upon his heads.

And his tail drew the third part of the stars of heaven, and did cast them to the earth . . .

And there was war in heaven: Michael and his angels fought against the dragon; and the dragon fought and his angels,

And prevailed not; neither was their place found any more in heaven.

And the great dragon was cast out, that old serpent, called the Devil, and Satan, which deceiveth the whole world: he was cast out into the earth, and his angels were cast out with him.

It is very likely that Lucifer had under his dominion one third of the angelic creatures, and these he led with him in rebellion against God. This was a celestial revolt.

Then shall he (the Lord) say also unto them on the left hand, Depart from me, ye cursed, into everlasting fire, prepared for the devil and his angels.

Matthew 25:41

Satan presents himself as a king of this host of spirits.

But when the Pharisees heard it, they said, This fellow doth not cast out devils, but by Beelzebub the prince of the devils.

And Jesus knew their thoughts, and said unto them, Every kingdom divided against itself is brought to desolation; and every city or house divided against itself shall not stand:

And if Satan cast out Satan, he is divided against himself; how shall then his kingdom stand?

Matthew 12:24-26

We must remember that God is a spirit, angels are spirits, and human beings are spirits clothed with bodies. These fallen spirits live in a negative world and are as angry with God and God's creation as the devil is. Therefore, we can only expect that their functioning will be very similar to Satan's. In fact, they carry out his wishes, his desires, and his commands. There are no ''good'' demon spirits; they are in complete subservience to their master, the devil.

6. Are there various kinds or categories of demons?

The Bible teaches us that demons have degrees of strength and authority. Jesus, speaking of epilepsy, said, *This kind goeth not out but by prayer and fasting* (Matt. 17:21). Here He was revealing that some demons are so strong that it takes the total surrender of the Christian in dedication and divine union with Christ to rebuke and loosen the evil spirit and to exorcise it from the possessed person.

There are demons who rule over large areas as lords, or leaders, and governors in the evil spirit world. For example, according to Buddhist belief, *Pa*, the ruling god of Singapore, demands that all his followers come first to his temple to burn incense and to worship him before they can go worship in any other of the many temples of the city. This is common knowledge among the Buddhists of that area.

Another example of demonic lordship is found in Calcutta, India, which is named after the female goddess, *Cali*. She is the ruling dignitary of the spirit world in that area. She is acknowledged and respected as the supreme ruler of that city.

Of course, a demon is neither male nor female; it is only the manifestation of that evil one who elects to be known as male or female.

In our discussion of the weaknesses or strengths of demon spirits, I find that a deaf spirit is the weakest and the easiest to dislodge and to bring forth from a person. Epilepsy is possibly the strongest to combat or to send forth. There are legions of different kinds of spirits. In my book, *Witch Doctor*, Mr. Arlindo Barbosa de Oliveira identified spirits and their relative strength as he dealt with them for over forty years as a witch doctor.

7. Where do demons live?

Demons principally live in the air above the earth because the devil is *the prince of the power of the air* (Eph. 2:2). It might be that they also have access to regions below the earth's surface. We do not know the extent of the territory or area over which they rule.

It could be possible that the headquarters of the devil is on the moon. There is no scripture to substantiate this theory, but we do know that the moon has a tremendous effect upon our earth. If someone goes crazy, he is called a lunatic, meaning "moon struck." Medical science has stated that patients in mental hospitals become very unstable during certain phases of the moon; they may be normal for twenty-eight days, then suddenly become stark raving mad. This is an area for further study.

Devils live in arid places. Jesus said, *When the unclean spirit is gone out of a man, he walketh through dry places* (Luke 11:24). Demons also live in evil places, places where crime and murders have been committed. (Rev. 2:13.) If you live in a house that seems foreboding or oppressive, either rebuke that threatening spirit in Jesus' name or sell the house and move out.

In the heathen world, demons have particular places they frequent—special cities or mountains or desert areas in which they live. Often they have certain trees which they inhabit. Some spirits may dwell in a special rock where the heathen come to worship them.

But, above all, demons wish to inhabit **humans.** In that way, they can give expression to their evil desires and unclean ways. (Matt. 8:28-34.)

8. What did Jesus personally say about the devil and demons?

Christ explained more about the activities of the devil and demons than did any other person in the scope of the Holy Scriptures.

It is very remarkable that Jesus Christ began His ministry with a confrontation with the devil. (Matt. 4:1-11.)

Christ spoke directly to the devil. (v. 4.)

Jesus recognized the devil's power. He did not say that the devil was lying when He was offered the nations of the world and its glory by him. (v. 8.)

Jesus resisted the devil by the Word of God. (v. 10.) Christ showed that the Word was the sword by which Christians overcome the devil.

Our Lord indicated that some forms of deafness are a spirit and also recognized dumbness as a spirit. (Mark 9:25.)

Christ called epilepsy (and other such seizures) a spirit. (Matt. 17:15-18.) The afflicted son spoken of in this passage was also called a lunatic. (v. 15.) These are symptoms which medical science may call sickness. Jesus Christ designated them as the work of evil spirits.

Even in the synagogue where Christ went to worship and to read from the Law of Moses, He discovered those who had evil spirits. In Luke 4:33, we read where Christ met a man with an unclean spirit. When the spirit cried out the identity of Jesus, that He was the Holy One of God, Jesus silenced the man and commanded the spirit to come out of him. In anger the spirit threw the man violently; but Christ would not let it hurt him, and the man was forever loosed of its power.

Christ at all times assumed complete strength and power over the demon forces, whether they were many as in the Gadarene demoniac of Mark 5:8,9, or one as in the woman of Luke 13:16 who had been tormented for eighteen years. At no time did Christ ever show any fear of demon forces or personalities. He declared, *All power is given unto me in heaven and in earth* (Matt. 28:18).

9. Did the twelve disciples of Jesus exorcise evil spirits?

One of the amazing things about the disciples is that they were ordinary men having followed ordinary vocations; but upon their spiritual relationship with Jesus Christ, they became men of dynamic divine power. When Jesus sent them forth, He commanded them to exercise divine power over evil spirits:

And when he had called unto him his twelve disciples, he gave them power against unclean spirits, to cast them out, and to heal all manner of sickness and all manner of disease.

Matthew 10:1

In Matthew 10:7,8, Christ issued a direct command to His disciples:

As ye go, preach, saying, The kingdom of heaven is at hand. Heal the sick, cleanse the lepers, raise the dead, cast out devils: freely ye have received, freely give.

These supernatural powers were the divine credentials of their office of apostleship. This is further substantiated in the Gospel of Luke:

Then he called his twelve disciples together, and gave them power and authority over all devils, and to cure diseases.

Luke 9:1

We find these disciples wonderfully carrying out this commission of their Lord and Savior. Christ also commissioned the second group of seventy disciples to go and preach:

After these things the Lord appointed other seventy also, and sent them two and two before his face into every city and place, whither he himself would come.

Therefore said he unto them, The harvest truly is great, but the labourers are few: pray ye therefore the Lord of the harvest, that he would send forth labourers into his harvest.

Luke 10:1,2

Then in verse 17 we read, *And the seventy returned again with joy, saying, Lord, even the devils are subject unto us through thy name.* These disciples were amazed at their ability to use the power of God to set captives free.

The final command Jesus gave to His disciples and the Church of all ages is found in Mark 16:15-17:

And he said unto them, Go ye into all the world, and preach the gospel to every creature. He that believeth and is baptized shall be saved; but he that believeth not shall be damned.

And these signs shall follow them that believe; In my name shall they cast out devils; they shall speak with new tongues.

This command has never been revoked or withdrawn. It challenges this generation today to use God's power to defeat the devil, just as it challenged the disciples the day Jesus gave the command.

10. Did the early Church fathers believe in or teach exorcism from demon power?

There is recorded history to support a positive response to this question. During the first centuries of the Christian Church, the spiritual leaders dealt extensively with demon power. Here are some examples:

Justin Martyr, in his apology *LIV*, insisted that heathen mythology was originated by demon power:

"The evil spirits were not satisfied with saying before Christ's appearance that those who were said to be sons of Jupiter were born of him: but after He had appeared and had been born among men, and when they learned how He had been foretold by the prophets and knew He should be believed upon and looked for in every nation, they again put forward other men, the Samaritans, Simon and Menander, who did mighty works by magic and deceived many and still kept them deceived."

From this quotation we see that Justin Martyr had a real grip on the functioning of demon power.

The Church father, Lactantius, in his *Divine Institutes, Number 2*, says:

"The inventors of astrology, and soothsaying, and divination, and those productions which are called oracles, and necromancy, and the art of magic, and whatever evil practices besides these men exercise, either openly or in secret: these are they who taught men from the worship of the true God, caused the countenances of dead kings to be erected and consecrated, and assumed to themselves their names."

The great Church father, Augustine, wrote in chapter 25 of his *City of God, Book 2*:

"What spirit can that be which by a hidden inspiration stirs men's corruption, and goads them into adultery, and feeds on full-fledged iniquity, unless it be the same that finds pleasure in such religious ceremonies, sets in the temples images of devils, and loves to see in play the images of vices;

that whispers in secret some righteous sayings to deceive the few who are good, and scatters in public invitations to profligacy, to gain possession of the millions who are wicked?''

In chapter 33 of his *Seventh Book*, Augustine rightly argues that Christianity, the only true religion, ''has alone been able to manifest that the gods of the nations are most impure demons, who desire to be thought gods, availing themselves of the names of certain defunct souls, or the appearance of mundane creatures, and with proud impurity divine honors, and envying human souls their conversion to the true God.''

The early Church fathers **did** believe in and preach against satanic forces. They taught the casting out, or exorcism, of demons; and they possessed Christ's power to deliver the afflicted from demonic forces.

It is modern theologians who have said little about demon power, and I find that the less preachers teach on demons, the more control the devil has over society. The Word of God says, *And the truth shall make you free* (John 8:32).

11. Why do demons wish to possess humans?

There is an age-long battle between God and the devil. As far as we know, the devil has no particular feeling for a human. The people who serve the devil faithfully for a lifetime do not receive any special honor or help from him. He shows no tenderness towards any human being. People throughout the world, who are totally demon possessed, are treated terribly by him. They become like animals, not like angels.

The only favors the devil shows are to people he is attempting to deceive or seduce. He lies to those who do not know his wicked designs.

The devil hates God Who cast him out of heaven. He cannot reach God to hurt Him personally because of His omnipotence; the only way he can injure God is to hurt and persecute

God's people. Those Christians who are the most dedicated to God, who love God with all their hearts, are the objects of Satan's vilest hatred.

The Christian believer has God loving him on one side, and the devil seeking to destroy him on the other. This results in the tremendous cosmic warfare which is now going on, invisible to the human eye.

Each person must choose to which of these forces he will surrender. Every human is either influenced by the power of God or the power of the devil.

Joshua, the great liberator of Israel, said, *Choose ye this day whom ye will serve* (Josh. 24:15). This means that man has the prerogative of choice. The devil cannot rule you or possess you without a yielding of your heart and mind to him.

Another reason that demons molest humans is that demons need a body in which to manifest their personalities. The highest place of occupancy is the human body. The human possessed by demon power does not display his true nature, but that of the spirit ruling him.

Also, the devil, who is the destroyed, wishes to take every human with him to hell. He is seeking whom he may destroy. (1 Pet. 5:8.)

12. Can a modern Christian have dominion and power over demons?

Yes, a born-again, Spirit-endowed Christian has dominion over devils.

Mathematics has its authority: rules, formulas, and equations.

Music has its authority: rules of harmony, time, and progression.

Christianity, too, possesses unique authority.

13. Just exactly what does this dominion involve? Where did we get it, and how do we use it?

The word *dominion* is from a Greek word *kurios*, which in New Testament usage means lordship, inherited rulership, and sovereignty.

Without knowledge of his true relationship with God, man cannot possess dominion over the many conflicts in life. Through the prophet Hosea, God tells us, *My people are destroyed for lack of knowledge* (Hos. 4:6).

Many Christians today do not realize their position of dominion. They belong to Christ; they are sons of God. Yet the devil keeps them in ignorance so they don't utilize their divine rights. Once they understand the basis of their dominion in Christ, they live a new life, attendant with power and victories.

If you were left a fabulous legacy by a loved one and did not know about it, you could live in abject poverty and perhaps die of starvation while actually possessing great wealth. This is just as true in spiritual life. It is imperative that you know—and know that you know—your rights as a follower of the Lord Jesus Christ. **You** are entitled to dominion.

Jesus exhibited dominion in every stage of His life. His virgin birth transcends the known laws of nature.

He began His earthly ministry by turning water into sparkling wine without the fermentation process. He further demonstrated dominion over the laws of nature by walking on the water, by multiplying bread and fish to feed the hungry, and by calming the tempestuous sea with a word. Christ showed His dominion over sickness and disease by never failing to heal those brought to Him. He even asserted dominion over the grave by rising from the dead.

No one on this earth has ever lived and taught dominion as Jesus did. He concluded His earthly ministry by declaring, *All power is given unto me in heaven and in earth* (Matt. 28:18). This is supreme dominion.

There is great dominion in the blood of Jesus. Christ came into this world for one splendid and glorious reason, and that was to shed His blood as a sacrifice for sin to save the human race. The Bible says that the life of the flesh is in the blood; therefore, it had to be His blood which was shed. Christ said to His disciples, *This is my blood . . . which* is shed for many for the remission of sins (Matt. 26:28). The holy, saving blood of Jesus has power and dominion.

There is remarkable dominion in the book we call the Bible. It is the only living Book among men, possessing great power to preserve itself and to bless all humanity. I accept the Bible as God's inspired Word. I believe with the writer of Hebrews that *the word of God is quick* (living), *and powerful, and sharper than any twoedged sword, piercing even to the dividing asunder of soul and spirit, and of the joints and marrow, and is a discerner of the thoughts and intents of the heart* (Heb. 4:12).

God has placed His Word in an exalted position above faith, or works, or human goodness. The Psalmist David said, . . . *for thou hast magnified thy word above all thy name* (Ps. 138:2).

Let God's Word be true; and every doubt, every fear, every fancy, every opinion, and every contrary circumstance be a liar. You must not base your faith on moral or spiritual improvement or feelings, which at times are most unreliable. Faith must be based on God's Word. **There is dominion in His Word.**

The Holy Spirit is also an important link in the chain through which dominion extends to the believer. The Holy Spirit has dominion—the power to do great miracles. He can move, and no one can hinder. As the third member of the Triune God, He knows no limit in time, energy, or space. He is the Comforter; He guides the believer; He convicts the sinner of sin. He is the Spirit of Truth.

Through the divine operation of the Holy Spirit, the disciple can possess dominion. He becomes the final link in the chain of command. The Lord Jesus Christ perpetuated dominion on earth by giving power to His disciples: *Behold, I give unto you power to tread on serpents and scorpions, and over all the power of the enemy: and nothing shall by any means hurt you* (Luke 10:19). Great Church leaders throughout history have exerted dominion as they lived victorious lives and set their fellow men free from the power of the devil.

Surrounded by such an array of glorious power and having association with such amazing strength, it is only reasonable that the disciple of Christ should be a partaker of this vast glory and that he, too, should enjoy this dominion.

Dominion—Lost and Found

Today, millions of human beings live in mental, spiritual, and physical bondage. Their number increases fearfully every day. As never before in history, insidious forces seek to degrade human dignity. Untold millions of men and women are held in these invisible chains, bound by fear and various evil habits which torment their lives and by awful diseases which crush them.

In primitive lands, all manner of base superstitions enslave the individual. Day and night he is frightened by witchcraft and unseen enemies. In modern society, it is oppressions and depressions which torment millions of men and women. The question naturally arises, *Why?* Why is mankind enmeshed in this awful bondage? To find an answer, we must go directly to the account of the creation of man recorded in the Word of God.

How was man created? For what purpose? Genesis 1:27,28 provides the answer:

So God created man in his own image, in the image of God created he him; male and female created he them.

And God blessed them, and God said unto them, Be fruitful, and multiply, and replenish the earth, and subdue it: and have dominion . . . over every living thing that moveth upon the earth.

Here God revealed that man was a created being, made in His image and after His likeness. God's love toward Adam is indicated in these words: *God blessed them.* His best wishes were indicated when He said, *Be fruitful, and multiply.* Adam's position on this earth was forever settled when God said, *Subdue it: and have dominion. . . over every living thing that moveth upon the earth.* This was man's beginning and his position with God.

With such an illustrious beginning—demonstrating lordship over the entire Garden of Eden, possessing credentials of rulership from the Most High—how could man have fallen into the quagmire of degradation, into slavery to Satan?

Man lost his freedom willfully and deliberately. Through his fall, he caused the entire world to fall with him. On the same day Adam transgressed against God, he died spiritually. Fear was born in his heart. He hid himself from God among the trees because he was afraid. That day physical mortification began, and Adam started to die. The spirit of Adam fell and he was separated from God, the Great Spirit. The highest part of his complex being had lost dominion. He was now wearing the devil's chains of slavery. What a change! With great dignity Adam had worn God's vested authority. Just as fish were created to swim, dogs were made to hunt, worms were made to crawl, so man was made to rule.

Man either has dominion or is under domination. He cannot be neutral. Man was created to be dominated by no force except the Divine. He was created to be a conqueror over any power of influence before him.

When God saw the terrible collapse of man, He immediately set about to redeem man from his fallen state, to restore man's dominion which was lost because of sin. He accomplished this in one master stroke by giving His only begotten Son, the Lord Jesus Christ, to bring man back into a place of divine dominion.

Who Can Have Dominion?

Dominion belongs to every believer who will accept the responsibility for exerting it. Jesus said, *Behold, I give unto you power to tread on serpents and scorpions, and over all the power of the enemy: and nothing shall by any means hurt you* (Luke 10:19). He also said, *Verily I say unto you, Whatsoever ye shall bind on earth shall be bound in heaven: and whatsoever ye shall loose on earth shall be loosed in heaven* (Matt. 18:18).

After a person is converted, the devil seeks in every way possible to hide his position of authority from him. Satan knows that when the believer is aware of his privileges and power, he (Satan) will be completely defeated and his works destroyed.

An age-long strategy of the devil is to attack the believer in the area of confession. He knows a person will never rise above his confession. So he deceives the believer into confessing sickness, faults, and weakness, rather than making the promises of God his confession of faith. You are what you confess to be. The devil uses this means to keep you in bondage. Satan does not want you to confess dominion in Christ and victories by the blood. When you make these your confession, you exert dominion, authority, and power.

It is my observation that people don't like substitutes. For this reason, an automobile dealer will display a sign over his business which reads, "Authorized Dealer." The sign means that a consumer can expect factory-trained service for his car and the use of genuine parts—no substitutes.

In the spiritual world, Bible-believing Christians are "authorized dealers'' of God's dominion. They have what God wants this world to have. It would be most fitting, therefore, for the Church to put up a sign which reads, "Authorized Dealer of God's Spirit and Power.''

Dominion is not for the select few. **It is for every disciple of the Lord Jesus Christ.** It is for **you.** Begin now to assert the rights and privileges that are yours as a child of God. I have always encouraged the lay members of my church not only to pray for themselves, but also to pray for others who are sick. I teach them to expect a miracle from God.

Today I offer you the same advice. Dare to believe! Dare to receive! Put divine dominion into practice in your life. Start now!

14. Do demons have greater power in some geographical areas than in others?

While demon power is universal and found in all parts of the world, it definitely is stronger in areas where there is little or no resistance to the devil. Where there is no prayer or Bible reading, demon power reaches terrible proportions and results in strange manifestations.

For example, I have felt more of an evil, oppressive spirit in the country of Tibet than almost anywhere else I have traveled in the world. This is because there is virtually no resistance or opposition to satanic power there. Rather, many people have given themselves over to the devil, and many others actually worship demons. Tibet reminds me of Revelation 2:13: *I know . . . where thou dwellest, even where Satan's seat is.*

The devil is trying to increase his strength and take over America by taking prayer and Bible reading out of our schools and homes. Even many Christian homes today are giving the devil an open door by failing to have regular family devotions and Bible reading. The devil has no power to hurt people where prayer is being offered and where the blood of Jesus is accepted as protection and covering. We can have complete control over the devil's activities against us through total dedication, total consecration, and total application of the blood of Jesus.

15. What is the spirit of infirmity? How does it affect a person? How can you tell whether a person has a spirit of infirmity or a physical defect? Is it demon possession?

A spirit of infirmity is one of the devil's spirits. There are many types of these spirits, all of which cause sickness. The suffering caused by a spirit by infirmity is not a real physical illness and cannot be detected or treated by a physician.

The sickness caused by a spirit of infirmity may move all over the body. It may manifest itself as a backache, then a sick headache, or perhaps an upset stomach, or pain in the chest. No treatment is successful against it. No pills or shots bring relief from it. No doctor can determine what is wrong with the patient suffering from this malady. In fact, literally millions of people are being sent to psychiatrists by their doctors because the cause of their illness and suffering cannot be found.

Of course, the reason medical treatment is unsuccessful is because the source of the problem is spiritual. A person being attacked by a spirit of infirmity needs to be set free by the delivering power of Jesus. God wants to set people free from the infirmities of the devil.

I would say that a person with a spirit of infirmity who did not seek deliverance, but surrendered himself to the evil thing in his body, would certainly be moving toward complete domination by Satan. Instead, the sufferer should find a man of God to exercise divine authority and dominion over the devil's power, binding and rebuking the spirit of infirmity.

16. Can demons cause some disease?

Although all disease ultimately comes from Satan, not all disease is caused by demon power. If some disease came upon a person as a result of his neglecting his body, one could not say it was caused by a demon.

However, if the malady was accompanied by a manifestation of a strange spirit, we would know its origin was demonic.

There are certain diseases which I believe are demonic manifestations. One of these is cancer. The very appearance of cancer reveals that it is an evil thing—completely abnormal and unnatural. Other diseases, such as epilepsy, may also fall into this category.

The important thing to remember is that whatever your need—regardless of the cause—Christ is the answer. Definitions in this area are not absolutely necessary. Whether you are injured in an automobile accident or suffer from sickness, disease, or satanic oppression, Jesus can and will set you free.

17. Can demons bless a person as well as curse him?

The devil does not really bless—he pretends or promises to bless. Through spiritism, the devil may convince a person that he has made him well, but that person will become sick again by the power of the devil. A demonic blessing is only momentary. Actually, it is a lie in disguise.

The devil is a deceiver. He has no tenderness or compassion toward any human being. If you could visit the countries of the world where demon power is strongest, you would not find people being helped or blessed by demons. Instead, you would find multitudes of people starving to death and ravaged by disease. Those who are totally demon possessed, who have given themselves over completely to the devil, are treated worst of all.

Demons, which are those angelic beings which fell from heaven with Lucifer, wish to possess human beings for various reasons. First, having no body of their own, they desire a temporal dwelling place. Secondly, they possess humans in order to strike back at God. God is too great and powerful for them to attack directly, so in their hatred they turn to His greatest creation, mankind, and oppress and destroy them. Their purpose is not to bless man, but to destroy him. In this way they hope to hurt God.

The Bible expressly teaches that all good comes from God: *Every good gift and every perfect gift is from above, and cometh down from the Father* (James 1:17).

18. When a demon-possessed person dies, does the evil spirit leave the body and seek to possess another human being?

Yes, of course, they do! The same spirits who lived in the days of Jesus live today. There are numerous reports of demon spirits speaking and boasting about the famous people of history in whom they have previously lived.

The devil will move in and take over any neutral territory: Any human who does not resist his power may be subject to the indwelling of demonic power. In times past, almost every American mother was a praying mother, and the Bible was read in nearly every home. Today the Bible is hardly ever opened, and very little prayer is offered. Tragically, as a direct result, the devil is fast making inroads into America as the people turn away from God and lose their spiritual power and awareness.

American people do not know much about demon power, but the heathen in other lands certainly do. What we call superstition is often demon power, and the pagans know it. The devil can even move into Christian homes, I believe, through the quarreling of the parents, the fighting of the children, the violence and vileness of television and other media. Also, I believe many people pick up evil spirits by going to wrong places —places where they had no business going.

19. Can demons imitate God or angels?

They certainly can! Remember, demons are spiritual beings, exactly like angels, so they have spiritual qualities and powers, including perceptions and pervasion. In other words, they are sensitive to recognize other spirits, and they can easily make their presence felt.

Because the devil is a liar (the Bible says he is the father of lies) and a deceiver, he likes nothing better than to make people think that he is God doing certain things or speaking to them. Without question, when Moses and Aaron challenged the pharaoh's magicians, it was demon power that operated through the pharaoh's men enabling them to work certain wonders and miracles.

One time in Java a woman came up to me and said, "You have a black angel in you, and I have a white angel in me!" I immediately rebuked her, saying, "No, I have Jesus Christ in my life, and you are filled with the devil!"

A Christian soon learns that he must test and try the spirits to determine whether or not they are of God. A spirit that cannot stand praise to Jesus Christ and His shed blood is easily discernible. Also, the voice of God never leads us contrary to the Bible. When a spiritual "voice" suggests a deed or action that is contrary to the Word of God, that is a clear indication of demonic activity. One should rebuke and resist the devil at all times.

20. Is demon activity universal or local?

Demon power is universal. It may be found in any and every part of the world.

As I have mentioned before, the devil's power is stronger where there is no prayer and Bible reading. The reason for this is that Satan knows full well that he has no power to hurt people who plead the blood of Jesus as covering and who communicate with God in regular prayer.

21. Should a Christian fear demons?

Absolutely not! Throughout the Bible we are told of the power and dominion God has given to His children. To live in fear of the devil and his demons is to live far below one's privilege and authority as a Christian.

The Word of God declares:

And these signs shall follow them that believe; In my name shall they cast out devils.

Mark 16:17

All power is given unto me in heaven and in earth.

Matthew 28:18

He that believeth on me, the works that I do shall he do also; and greater works than these shall he do.

John 14:12

Resist the devil, and he will flee from you.

James 4:7

And the seventy returned again with joy, saying, Lord, even the devils are subject unto us through thy name.

And he said unto them, I beheld Satan as lightning fall from heaven.

Behold, I give unto you power to tread on serpents and scorpions, and over all the power of the enemy: and nothing shall by any means hurt you.

Luke 10:17-19

Fear is often the product of ignorance, of not knowing. People have a tendency to be afraid of anything they don't understand. Early-day map makers wrote on their charts over the unknown areas of the ocean, ''Dragons be here!''

Today, many Christians are afraid of demon power because they have been kept in ignorance about it. Because they do not understand their position of authority and power, many Christians are apprehensive and uneasy when they think of facing a supernatural power. Naturally, the devil seeks in every way possible to deceive the Christian and to bluff him into trembling, fearful subjection. He knows that the informed and prepared Christian can defeat him and destroy his works in every encounter.

Never be afraid of the devil. Because you are covered by the shed blood of Jesus Christ, you are invincible. You can defeat and triumph over the devil in every situation. **Remember, Satan is afraid of your authority, so use it to be victorious.**

22. **Jesus said that at the Judgment some would come to Him and say that they had done many wonderful works, casting out devils in His**

name. What did He mean by saying
that He would have to tell them,
"Depart from me: I never knew
you"?

We are not saved by our deeds or
good works. It is impossible to come to
a saving knowledge of our Lord Jesus
Christ except by the blood of the Lamb.
If Jesus says He does not know a person
at the Judgment, it is because that
person never was covered by Christ's
blood. There is no other means of
salvation.

As a matter of fact, there are many
who claim special power to heal and
deliver who are not blood-washed
Christians. Spiritualists and Christian
Scientists, as well as other cultists and
misguided individuals, have made great
claims of doing wonderful things in
Jesus' name. But because they are not
covered by the blood of Jesus, He will
say to them, "Depart from me: I never
knew you," when they face Him at the
Judgment.

23. Do the various kinds or categories
    of demons work together in

harmony? Do demons get along with each other?

Apparently not. Mr. Arlindo Barbosa de Oliveira, a Brazilian witch doctor for forty years, told me many amazing accounts of demon power. He identified spirits and listed them in categories of varying relative strength.

He said that the many ranks of devils are always fighting among themselves. He claims that he watched as two devils fought over his six-year-old brother. They were disputing about which one would possess him completely. Each demon said, "He is mine!" They fought over the youngster until the violence of their struggle killed him. The child was carried out and buried, an actual victim of demonic murder.

24. **When a demon is cast out, is there danger of it running amuck and harassing or possessing innocent persons present?**

No, there is no danger of an innocent person being troubled by an evil spirit as it is cast out. The person who exorcises a demon and sets the possessed individual free can also determine what the unseated spirit can and cannot do.

The Bible gives an excellent example of this in Matthew, chapter 8. Jesus cast out the devils from two men in the country of the Gergesenes. These were fierce devils, manifesting themselves through the men so violently that travelers could not even pass nearby without being attacked. Yet, when Jesus cast them out, the evil spirits pleaded and whined pitifully: *So the devils besought him, saying, If thou cast us out, suffer us to go away into the herd of swine* (Matt. 8:31).

Jesus had complete control over what the demons could do and where they could go. We have that same God-given authority.

25. Would a baby be safe where demons are being exorcised, as it has no power to resist evil?

Yes, I am sure that a baby or child would be quite safe. As I have said, the exerciser of demons can determine and control their destiny. Also youngsters up to the age of accountability are protected and covered by the blood of Christ. I cannot see where there would be any danger at all.

26. Do you think there is a connection between demon power and the spreading use of and addiction to narcotic drugs?

I am absolutely convinced that narcotics and drugs are major instruments of the devil's power today. If you remember that Satan is constantly striving to strike at God by attacking and hurting man, you can see how drugs such as LSD, "speed," amphetamines, and other addictive narcotics fit into this pattern. They bring nothing but misery, heartache, and suffering to every life they touch.

Also, the devil's traditional mode of operation is revealed in the pattern of drug use. People experiment with drugs because they have been promised a thrill, a "kick," an exciting and rewarding experience. For some, perhaps, at first it is. But soon the thrill is gone, and they must use more or stronger drugs, until finally they are hopelessly trapped, getting in deeper and deeper every day.

At first, the devil's promise of "good" seems to come true. Then, the whole thing rapidly becomes a hideous nightmare. What started out as a search for a "kick" leads to all sorts of evil—lies, thievery, robbery, lust, prostitution, murder, and anything else required of the addict. How the devil must mock and scorn to have a human so totally in his control!

In the countries of the world where demon power is strongest, you will find thousands of people using drugs. In China, Tibet, India, Indonesia, and other countries, narcotics and strong drugs are used in weird, unearthly worship rituals to demons and idol gods.

I have walked through dark, narrow alleys in Hong Kong littered with the sprawled, emaciated bodies of suffering, dying addicts. The air was so heavy with the smoke and stench of burning opium and hashish that I could hardly get my breath. You could look into the tortured faces and tormented eyes of these people and see that they were demon possessed. My flesh crawled with the overwhelming sensation of evil. My spirit told me unmistakably that the devil's power was strong all around.

I have seen the same look on the faces of young people in this country who have given themselves over to drugs. You see, drugs take control of the mind and spirit. This allows the devil to move in; it gives him a free hand to possess and control a person's entire being.

Many young people are being deceived and trapped by Satan through narcotics in our country today. Soon they find themselves in the grip of something from which they can't break away. It is more than a physical craving or appetite. It is a spirit!

That's why there is no medical cure for addiction. The addict may seem to be off drugs and perfectly normal, then he just goes berserk for no apparent reason. Addicts need to be delivered and set free from the demonic power of the devil. There is no other cure.

One more thing: The people who push drugs, selling them to youngsters and even children, are definitely demon possessed. They know the terrible consequences of their hellish product, yet they entice and seduce others, sometimes innocent people, into partaking of the poison that will ruin their lives. These are the most cruel, most despicable people on the face of the earth. Their action is not normal or natural at all. It is the work of the devil. Their only hope is deliverance from demon power through a man of God with great spiritual power and authority.

27. How can we recognize symbols of demon power?

There are two areas of supernaturalism: demon power and God's power. God warns us against all kinds of supernaturalism not of Him. Thus, anything at all related to the devil's power should have no relationship with us.

What say I then? that the idol is any thing, or that which is offered in sacrifice to idols is any thing?

But I say, that the things which the Gentiles sacrifice, they sacrifice to devils, and not to God: and I would not that ye should have fellowship with devils.

1 Corinthians 10:19,20

The great Apostle Paul says that idols are nothing, and even the offerings to them are nothing. But behind every idol is a demon that craves worship. The idol is only a symbol. Behind that symbol is the devil's power.

You would be astounded to see what our team witnesses when we go out in our public meetings and crusades. Time after time we see terrible manifestations in people who are actually bound by the devil simply because they cherish symbols of demon power. We are seeing more of it in a single three-day meeting now than we once saw over a five-year period! The battle is on for men's immortal souls — and we are ready to do battle with the devil, bringing the power of God and the anointing of the Holy Spirit against any power at Satan's command.

Let me say that symbols are not unusual. God has always had symbols of His power. In the Old Testament, we read about the Ark of the Covenant. The Ark was a symbol of God's power, and it was placed in the Holy of Holies. Above the Ark was the Shekinah—a light unlike any human light. There were no electric lights, no candles, no artificial light of any kind in the Holy of Holies; but a glow, a wondrous radiance, shone forth from the Ark of God. The Ark was a symbol of God's power and presence with His people. Whenever the Shekinah was gone, then God was gone. The Ark was simply a symbol of His power.

The heathen did not understand this. When the Philistines captured the Ark, knowing it was a religious object, they put it in their temple. Next morning, their own god, Dagon, was down on his face, broken in pieces, destroyed. Nothing but the presence of God in the symbolic Ark could do that.

The devil also has symbols of his power. And you had better take notice of them. As Christians, we should not have symbols of the devil's power in our possession. These symbols may have strength you don't know about. So, you should be careful with them and about them.

The heathen have all kinds of symbols of the devil's power. The witch doctors of Haiti have little dolls they have made for themselves—awful-looking little things. By sticking pins through these dolls, they can actually cause injury to people at great distances from themselves. These little dolls become symbols of the power of witchcraft. You might say that these symbols couldn't have any strength or power. You may not understand it at all. But this vicious system does work. It is demon power.

All the voodoo religions have artifacts. They have all kinds of good-luck charms and many different symbols that represent the power of the devil.

When I was in China a number of years ago, I remember visiting a Buddhist temple and allowing the priest there to show me their gods. They had a fantastic array of idol gods—ugly ones, big ones, frightening ones. They even had gods with eight or ten arms.

I looked up at an especially big one that was about sixteen or eighteen feet tall, and I said, "Surely, you know that thing can't do anything for you."

He was very polite. He smiled and said, "You are a foreigner. You just don't understand."

"Well," I said, "tell me how it can do anything."

The priest said, "Of course, we all know that an idol does not have any power. But the spirit that lives in that idol certainly does. The spirit of that idol is off wandering around somewhere right now. If I were to bring some incense and an offering, and place it in front of the idol, something would start happening immediately."

Then he took me around to the back of the idol and showed me a hole cut into its back.

He said, ''That is where the spirit goes in and out. When someone comes here to worship the idol, then the spirit runs and get inside, because it wants worship. If people come and kneel here with an offering, burning candles and incense before this idol, then immediately the spirit is here and he does things for people. You are just ignorant of what he can do.''

Well, I want you to know I had a pretty strange feeling! Suddenly, I realized that the idol was only the symbol of a demonic spirit. The grotesque-looking face of that idol was something an artisan created under the influence of the devil's power. The idol had become a symbol of the devil's influence and power over the lives of the people in that place.

The devil wants to be worshiped, and he will get into any kind of idol if you will come and worship him there. You wouldn't want one in your house, and I wouldn't want one in mine. Why would we want the symbol of the devil's power around us?

In the Filipino headhunter country where we have helped build churches, there is a village with a special tree. It doesn't have a leaf on it, not one! It makes you feel strange to look at the thing. It is greasy. I suppose that is because so many people have wiped their hands on it for years. When you look at the tree, there is something about it that is odd. Even the boughs are crooked and gnarled. It is an awful-looking thing. It looks as if it is possessed.

That tree is a symbol of demon power. The tribesmen say that spirits are in that tree, so they offer sacrifices and burn incense at the foot of it. They come to meet the devil at this symbol of his evil power. They say things happen at that tree that can happen nowhere else!

In Manila, Philippines, we prayed for a prison girl named Clarita who was being attacked by demons. While we were praying for her, we observed that she had a very strange metal cross hanging around her neck. For her, that cross was a symbol of the devil's power.

Clarita often acted just like an animal. One day during questioning in the office of the Chief of Police, she fell to the floor and crawled under the desk.

The chief kicked her and said, "Come out from under there!"

She crawled out and began to whine, "I've lost my cross."

He told her he didn't know anything about her cross. He even turned his pockets inside out and said, "You see, I don't have it."

She looked at him with a strange look and said, "Look again."

Disgusted, he plunged his hand back into his pocket. The metal cross was there! It almost scared him to death. Less than thirty seconds after he had his hands in those pockets, and even had them wrong-side out shaking them, the cross appeared inside!

While in Indonesia, we stayed in the home of a witch doctor. He wasn't an important witch doctor; he only had seven devils. Most of them have many more than that. While he was at work one day, his wife said she would show us how he communicated with his spirits. The spirits he worshiped were so wicked they wouldn't even let her stay in the same room with him. She had to sleep in another room. When she tried to sleep with her husband, these spirits violently threw her onto the floor. She had black and blue marks all over her body.

You may not understand things like that, but a lot of people in America are beginning to see things about the devil's power they never understood before.

When we entered the witch doctor's room, I saw a fine wire, possibly made of silver or gold, hanging from the ceiling. Suspended at the end of this wire was a beautiful dagger, which slowly moved back and forth. The woman told me that when her husband came here to worship, he knelt on a raised place in the floor, like a low altar, and burned incense. As the smoke rose up and around this dagger, all the spirits he worshiped came around him.

She said, "You ought to hear it. Sometimes all of them are talking at the same time, and it sounds like a whole congregation chattering away. We can hardly stay in the house when they are having a conference in that room."

This witch doctor contacted the demons through the dagger. That was the symbol of the devil's power.

Clairvoyants may use other symbols of the devil's power, such as a crystal ball or a deck of cards, to tell a person about his life and his future.

I must warn you that you may have in your own home emblems of the devil's power. Perhaps you don't understand why certain things are happening to you there. Maybe you need to have a "housecleaning."

You say, "Well, what could we have?" It might be that you have a Ouija board. If you do, take it out and burn it in Jesus' name. It is a symbol of Satan's power.

It may be that you have some professional playing cards. Almost every witch doctor and fortune-teller in the whole world uses them. They help them in their business. If that be true, you have no business with them in your house!

Maybe you have a crystal ball. It might be a toy or a plaything, but it shouldn't be in your home. You ought to destroy it!

On the whatnot shelf you may have some little idols. You can buy almost any heathen idol in the department stores in America today. Our country has been flooded with all kinds of idol dolls, Buddhas, etc. I had one in my office, and we took a picture of that thing getting its head smashed. That little statue had been sent to us by a Full Gospel Christian. We appreciated the person's thinking that we would like it and sending it all the way from Hong Kong, but we don't want an idol sitting around in our office. We destroyed it!

You may have some curios that you brought from foreign lands, and have them sitting around your house. In many homes I have seen Buddhas, Confucius dolls, and different heathen idols. I don't believe they should be in the home of a Christian. I believe we should clean them out, in the name of Jesus.

In the Old Testament the people were very careful about pictures, images, and such things. In some parts of the world people are still careful about pictures. For example, an Orthodox Jew does not like to have his picture taken. If you want to start a quarrel in Jerusalem, find an Orthodox Jew with his long beard and traditional clothes, and try to photograph him. You will have trouble on your hands. He believes it is a sin to have that symbol or image of him in your camera or in your hands.

As you know, the Amish people in this country also do not want their pictures taken and do not allow pictures in their homes. They do not want any symbol around that could cause people to move into idolatry or that would give the devil any chance to move into their homes.

Let us look at Acts 19:19:

Many of them also which used curious arts brought their books together, and burned them before all men: and they counted the price of them, and found it fifty thousand pieces of silver.

At that time, 30 pieces of silver was the price of a slave. One piece of silver was a full day's wage for a craftsman. This means that with 50,000 pieces of silver one could have purchased 1,666⅔ slaves. There was no man in the empire wealthy enough to own that many slaves.

If one piece of silver was a craftsman's pay for one day, then there were represented here a total of 50,000 days, or 137 years, of work.

Now you begin to realize the magnitude and the significance of what these people did. They brought untold wealth into the streets and burned it. They destroyed it publicly, so that nothing was left. Why? Because these books represented the devil's power, and the people wanted to rid themselves of any trace of contamination by demonic forces.

If destroying the symbols of the devil's power was so important and necessary then, I believe it is no less important now. We must learn to recognize all symbols of demon power and be sure to give them no place in our lives.

28. Does a person possessed of an evil spirit receive his salvation before or after his deliverance?

This is a very unusual question. The answer, I believe, lies in determining what state the demon-possessed person is in at the time of deliverance. For example, if one were possessed of a spirit of jealousy or a spirit of lying, he would have to accept God's means of salvation first. However, if he had a deaf or dumb spirit, he could easily understand the salvation message through an interpreter.

On the other hand, if one were possessed of devils, as the demoniac of Gadara, his thinking would be so impaired and controlled by Satan that he would have no mind or ability to accept salvation. The demoniac of Gadara had no capacity of will power. He lived in the cemetery. He tore his clothes off his body. He cut himself with sharp stones. He broke every rope and chain put on him. It was necessary for him to receive his deliverance first; then, clothed and in his right mind, he was able to sit at the feet of Jesus and worship his Savior.

The ex-demoniac with his new mind begged Jesus for permission to travel with Him as a disciple, but Jesus told him to go back to his own family and testify of the divine deliverance he had received.

It should be stated that soul salvation and spiritual deliverance are very closely associated. Jesus said to the one healed of lameness, *Behold, thou art made whole: sin no more, lest a worse thing come unto thee* (John 5:14). He says this to all who receive His miracle power of deliverance in spirit or body.

29. Can evil spirits live in a building such as a house? How do they get there? How can one get them out?

Yes, an evil spirit can live in any place where it is welcomed or any place where it can assume authority and not be hindered.

Fallen angel spirits feel they must communicate with man. This is because they are part of the fallen group which were cast out of heaven and which also caused the fall of Adam in the Garden of Eden. These evil spirits will seek to dominate a total community or area. They will make their homes in any place where they will be respected or worshiped.

It is well known that evil spirits inhabit houses. There are many houses in which there are heard shouts, loud footsteps, voices, etc. Many times these noises are accompanied by all kinds of evil apparitions and disturbances. I have helped to deliver people from such demonic activity in their homes.

As to the second question, how do evil spirits get into buildings, oftentimes it is through very evil people who live in such places. Other times, it is because of some terrible accident or happening which has taken place there. It may be that a person who was possessed of a spirit had lived in the house and afterwards it would still be affected by that sinister presence.

As for the third part of the question, how does one get rid of these spirits, let me say that if you don't get rid of them, then move out. But if a person has the ministry of deliverance, he does not have to move; he moves the devil.

If you should encounter this situation, turn the house into a place of prayer meetings for God's people to come and pray and sing. Then have the minister in and ask him to anoint the house and pray over it, exorcising every evil force within its limits. Many such houses have been cleansed from such spirits by the power of God. I trust you will have immediate deliverance.

30. **Does a person have to permit a devil to enter him, or can the devil enter anyone he wishes?**

This subject is dealt with more fully in Question 38. In response, I must begin on the positive side and say that God's children have power over every evil. Jesus Christ stated and restated this truth.

Evidently, there are many avenues by which the devil can enter into a person. For example, if a person permits his temper to go astray until he screams uncontrollably, he opens his spirit at that moment for demon possession. When this spirit of rage possesses a person, it might induce him to lie and the spirit of lying would come to abide with him. These spirits might urge him to steal and the spirit of theft would possess him. He would really not know why he stole or why he lied; he would only know that a strange urge from deep within made him do it.

In the beginning, in most instances, a person has to open the doors to his mind and spirit for an evil force to enter and possess him. He can be freed from such possession by the authority and power of Jesus Christ when exorcised by a Holy Spirit-anointed servant of Christ.

When any person becomes aware that the devil has taken advantage of him, he should immediately seek complete deliverance.

31. Who can cast out devils? How does one know when he can cast out devils?

In considering this question, we must determine who gave the commission or the command to cast out devils and to whom it was given. It was Jesus Christ Who commissioned His first twelve apostles to go and cast out devils. (Matt. 10:1,7,8; Luke 9:1.)

Later when His seventy apostles returned to Him, they were rejoicing that even the devils were subject to them by the pronouncing of His name against them. (Luke 10:17.)

In Acts 1:8, Jesus said that His disciples would receive power after the Holy Spirit had come upon them. Power would be useless if it were not brought against interfering and un-Christian attitudes and spirits.

In the Great Commission of Mark 16:15-17, the Lord Jesus said:

Go ye into all the world, and preach the gospel to every creature. He that believeth and is baptized shall be saved; but he that believeth not shall be damned.

And these signs shall follow them that believe; In my name shall they cast out devils . . . .

The Lord Jesus specifically said that those who believe would cast out devils. Of course, these are persons who believe and accept the Gospel. They personally know God's power and have become holy vessels unto God. They accept by faith the sign ministry and therefore exorcise evil spirits.

This simply means that the casting out of spirits does not belong especially to the hierarchy. It does not belong uniquely to bishops or men of ecclesiastical position. The Bible specifically says that those who exercise faith have this power to relieve those who are tormented by spirits.

I feel that it is always best to stick only to what the Word of God says about such matters. Church doctrines and church disciplines could lead a person to a non-biblical position toward those who need divine deliverance.

32. What specific names does the Bible give to demon spirits?

There are a host of names used in God's Word to identify evil spirits. Our Lord Jesus used a number of them.

Here is a short list of these with references:

1. *Spirit of infirmity* (Luke 13:11).
2. *Dumb and deaf spirit* (Mark 9:25).
3. *Unclean spirit* (used 22 times) (Matt. 12:43; Mark 1:23; Luke 9:42).
4. *Blind spirit* (Matt. 12:22).
5. *Familiar spirits* (Lev. 20:27; Is. 8:19; 2 Kings 23:24).
6. *An angel of light* (2 Cor. 11:14).
7. *A lion* (1 Pet. 5:8).
8. *A dragon* (Rev. 12:7-9).

9. *A lying spirit* (used 4 times)
   (1 Kings 22:22,23; 2 Chron.
   18:21,22).

10. *Seducing spirits* (1 Tim. 4:1).

11. *Binding spirit* (Matt. 18:18).

12. *A foul spirit* (used 2 times)
    (Mark 9:25; Rev. 18:2).

13. *Jealous spirit* (used 2 times)
    (Num. 5:14,30).

Very often evil spirits give themselves names. One told me that he was the "serpent spirit." Another said loudly, "I am the angel over blood."

We must at all times keep in mind that Christ Jesus gave His disciples power and authority over **all** devils. (Matt. 10:1-8; Luke 9:1-6.)

33. Is fasting or praying important in exorcising spirits? Can some be cast out without fasting while others cannot?

As Jesus Christ is our chief example and we are exhorted to follow Him, we should consider that the Bible repeatedly says Christ fasted often. I personally believe that fasting is a source of spiritual strength and power.

Just before Christ's triumphant entry into His public ministry, He fasted for forty days. It seems that our Master fasted before the major experiences in His life.

For us today, it is very important to fast, especially before seeking to cast out some evil spirits.

We are taught that there are varying powers of demonic force in the spirit world. After casting out the epileptic spirit from the boy who had thrown himself in the fire and into the water, Christ told His disciples that they could not cast it out because *this kind goeth not out but by prayer and fasting* (Matt. 17:21). Therefore it is sure that there are certain spirits who will resist until one has prepared himself for spiritual encounter.

Personally, every great victory I have experienced in the casting forth of spirits has been after a time of fasting and prayer. For instance, I remember the girl in the Philippines, Clarita Villanueva, who was bitten by devils. I refused to minister to her until I had spent time before God fasting and praying. I went to see the mayor of Manila and also the head doctor of Bilibid Prison to get permission to pray for her, then set a subsequent date to return and pray for her. I felt that I needed time in fasting and prayer before ministering to her. It became evident that the spirit would not have moved had I not spent this time in prayer before God with fasting.

Also, there was the case of the boy in Manila called the "Invisible Boy," who mysteriously appeared and disappeared. I fasted for him, beseeching God to relieve him of this awful spirit. He remains free until this day.

As a final example, there was Mr. Go Puan Seng, a Chinese friend who owns a newspaper in Manila. He asked me to pray for his daughter who was suffering from an evil spirit. I told him that I would fast and pray for two days before going to his house. When we prayed for God to set her free, she was immediately released from the devil's power.

In my own experience I have found it imperative to fast and pray before seeking to set a person free from demon power.

34. Is adultery an evil spirit?

In my dealing with spiritual phenomena, I find that when one surrenders his will power to any evil, that thing comes to possess him. He becomes a slave to it. He cannot do as he wishes anymore, but must obey that particular evil. (Rom. 6:16.)

No doubt one of these evils is adultery. If a person gives his mind constantly to moral abuse and immoralities, a spirit enters and drives him into deep sin. He often says and does things against his will because of the strength of this evil which has come to possess him.

In such a case of possession, the only way this person can be set free is for the minister of God to use Christ's authority and power to exorcise this unclean spirit.

A terrible result of such an evil taking hold upon a person is that it becomes a doorkeeper to his soul and spirit. It can now bring other evil spirits into that life. For example, a person can surrender to stealing and become a kleptomaniac. He will steal impulsively, even though he does not need what he takes. This spirit becomes a doorkeeper spirit in that soul. It can permit the spirit of lying to come in. When that happens, the person will impulsively lie about anything, even when the truth would sound better.

Jesus taught this truth in Luke 11:24-26 when He said that the evil spirit which was cast out from a man found no rest. It wandered in dry places. When it returned, it found the house (the man's soul) swept, garnished, and empty. This spirit reoccupied this man, bringing with it seven more demons who were even more evil than itself.

Christ said that the last state of that man was worse than before he was delivered of the demon spirit. This simply means that a person who submits to evil such as adultery lays himself open to receive other evils that the devil wishes to place upon him. By all means, we must keep ourselves free from all the devil's power!

35. How much knowledge of any existing situation does an evil spirit have?

The Word of God is the only source of knowledge in this area. The Bible teaches us that God knows the thoughts of mankind completely. First Chronicles 28:9 says, . . . *the Lord searcheth all hearts, and understandeth all the imaginations of the thoughts.*

In many scriptures we are taught that God understands the total thinking capacity of man. I believe that God is the only one with power to completely enter into the innermost being of a person and determine his thought life. The devil might be able to pick up a smattering here or there, and even humans sometimes pick up a thought from another person by E.S.P. (extrasensory perception). However, a consistent survey of the Bible proves that only God fully knows the thought life of a human being. Satan functions on obtainable knowledge and upon prophecies that he has heard.

I believe that we should protect our world of thought. We should have it cleansed by the blood of the Lord Jesus and completely sanctified, for it is out of man's heart and thought life that proceeds either good or evil.

To have total victory in thought and speech is to have victory in the total Christian experience.

A person's mind is his strongest possession in which to either resist the devil or to submit to the great will and purposes of God.

The devil is limited in his knowledge, but he is not limited in his lies, deceptions, and frauds. The Bible tells us to *try the spirits* (1 John 4:1).

36. **I live in constant fear of sinning against the Holy Spirit and of losing my mind. Could this fear be a tormenting spirit?**

In answer to this question, let me first stress that fear of any type is wrong and is of satanic origin. What we must realize is that the Bible says the devil is the accuser of the brethren. (Rev. 12:10.) Many people are fearful of sinning against the Holy Spirit when there is no reason for such fear. To sin against the Holy Spirit, a person's total spirit, soul, and body must turn violently against the Bible and hate God. This really means that not many people have committed this unpardonable and unforgivable sin.

The second fear, that of losing one's mind, is also one which torments many people unnecessarily. Since God never torments anyone in this way, it is easy to discern that it is Satan who brings such destroying thoughts. As I have stated previously, fear has no rational basis. This is seen very clearly in this case. When you are attacked by fear, you are not losing your mind, neither are you sinning against the Holy Spirit. When that happens, you should obey what the Apostle James says: *Resist the devil, and he will flee from you* (James 4:7).

A tormenting spirit can only go as far as permitted. It is up to you to take action against it.

Once Rev. Kenneth Hagin, wishing to pray for a person for deliverance, could see a small devil between him and the sick person. This devil was making all kinds of noises and jumping about hysterically, trying to keep Brother Hagin from getting deliverance for the woman. He prayed, "Lord, remove this thing." To which the Lord replied, "**You** move it. **You** command it to go." When he did, the spirit was instantly gone and the person for whom he was praying was delivered.

You must not permit the devil to torment you through lies. Our souls are perfectly secure through the blood of Jesus Christ. Paul assures us, *God hath not given us the spirit of fear; but of power, and of love, and of a sound mind* (2 Tim. 1:7).

You have a divine right to claim a sound mind and certainly God will grant it to you.

37. Can superstition be an evil spirit?

Superstition thrives under certain conditions. It has to have the proper climate to flourish. Naturally, a spiritually starved and morally bankrupt society produces the best ground for superstition. A man without God turns to superstition for release of tensions and to seek after forbidden knowledge.

Superstition was born because man in his deepest being longs for the supernatural. The soul of man rejects the wholly materialistic way of life. The immortal soul becomes starved for spiritual food when fed philosophy, scientific facts, and religious ritualism. It instinctively seeks release in the unknown. Devoid of truth and life in Christ, foolish and stupid ideas are formed and taught as fact.

Superstition is a confusion between truth and falsehood. People who are superstitious are actually seeking after truth. A man of faith does not inquire of the stars to find God's will for his life. He knows the will of God. He trusts his future to Christ.

Superstitious magic has many facets. One of these is luck. Multitudes are looking for luck. People seek it in metal, stones, jewels, and rabbit's feet. They trust in lucky charms or lucky days as they seek for something supernatural. In so doing, they discover that luck has two aspects—good luck and bad luck. They say that if one breaks a mirror it will bring him seven years of bad luck. This superstition goes back to the time when people believed that a reflection of the soul is seen in a mirror and that this reflection is a part of a person's soul. When the mirror is accidentally broken, it brings bad luck to the one whose soul image was reflected there.

A Christian does not believe in luck—bad or good. The Bible teaches us that every good and perfect gift comes from God. The devil brings us nothing. All that we have is the good gift from God for which we give thanks.

Reading horoscopes is not anything new. Millions have sold their souls as slaves to the movement of the stars. Sad to say, some Christians go to their newspapers to find out the positions of the stars and to seek advice and guidance through the reading of the horoscope. It is their belief that the position of the heavenly bodies affects people's lives. For example, a person born under the sign of the planet Mars is supposed to have a violent disposition because Mars was the Roman god of war.

The Bible is opposed to all superstition. In the Book of Leviticus God warns us:

Regard not them that have familiar spirits, neither seek after wizards, to be defiled by them . . .

And the soul that turneth after such as have familiar spirits, and after wizards, to go a whoring after them, I will even set my face against that soul, and will cut him off from among his people.

Leviticus 19:31; 20:6

Palmistry is gaining favor today. It is big business. Palm readers say that the palm of a human being can reveal the future of that person.

The Bible clearly says that anything which takes a person's interest away from God as the Source of **all** supernatural power and which causes him to look elsewhere for the supernatural is idolatry. You cannot place your trust in any source except God.

The grave danger of superstitions lies in opening one's mind to seek this knowledge, then opening the spirit and soul to receive it. The true Christian will not entrust his hand to a gypsy or anyone else to have his future foretold. Yet at this very moment, America is permitting heathen witch doctors and pagan gurus who claim to have supernatural powers to come and spread their lies among the people.

In my living in over 100 nations of the world for many years, I have come to know the deep fears in the hearts of the heathen. They are afraid of God and of demons. They are afraid of the dead and of departed spirits. They live in mortal fear of the unknown and of the future. They are tortured by a multiplicity of superstitions handed down to them from one generation to another.

God's Word says in 1 John 4:18, . . . *fear hath torment.* Superstitious fears can ruin your health. A businessman once went to the doctor because he was nervous, frustrated, and on the verge of mental collapse. The doctor talked with him and found that he was not in any financial distress nor did he have a domestic problem. Through counseling, the doctor finally discovered that the man was an ardent believer in astrology and read everything he could about his horoscope. He explained to the doctor that because of the opposition of Mars and Saturn and the unfavorable position of the moon, he was proven to be incurable!

How difficult to believe that a succesful businessman would permit his mind to become so twisted with superstitious astrology. Even when the medical doctor could find nothing wrong with this otherwise seemingly rational man, he still believed his condition to be incurable because of the position of the planets.

The Christian is fully protected from all demon power and from every superstition. Let me list six means of divine protection, as outlined in God's Holy Word, which are available to us as believers:

1. *The Word of God.* God's Word is strong armor. The Bible is divine and eternal truth. Therefore, the revealed Word of God possesses power to counteract superstition and to destroy it in every form.

2. *The blood of Jesus.* There is security in the shed blood of Christ. Through it Christians have divine power over superstition.

3. *The authority of the believer.* In His Great Commission, our Lord Jesus Christ Himself said that those who believe shall cast out devils. (Mark 16:17.) The Christian is secure because of this divine authority invested in him.

4. *The Holy Spirit.* I find from my own personal experiences that spiritism and superstition have no place in a Spirit-filled life. Jesus promised us that the Holy Spirit would lead us into all truth. (John 16:13.) Thank God, the

blessed Holy Spirit reveals that truth to us and separates it from all error.

5. *The gifts of the Spirit.* Another tremendous safety factor against superstition is the functioning of the gifts of the Holy Spirit in the Church. (1 Cor. 12.) The truth destroys error!

6. *Prayer.* To receive an instantaneous answer to prayer is a miracle. This intimate relationship with God leaves no place for absurd superstitions.

In conclusion, I feel that witchcraft and superstitions are damning powers for a nation or a person.

Deliverance begins by being born again of the Spirit of God and receiving a new nature. In Ephesians 2:1 the Apostle Paul writes: *You hath he quickened, who were dead in trespasses and sins.* We have been revived or resurrected by God's mighty power. This is the greatest function of supernatural power in the universe.

38. Could a schizophrenic be considered demon possessed?

I would say it is probable that a schizophrenic is tormented by the devil. Schizophrenia is certainly an abnormal mental condition. Often the schizophrenic exhibits a dual personality.

Often we know what a thing is by what it does. Does a schizophrenic love God and show it? Is he as sociable as other members of his family? Does he rise to high levels of achievement? Is he a blessing to his community? The answers to these questions help identify schizophrenia.

Schizophrenia has no apparent benefits for anybody. This reveals to us that it is not of God. I've never known a person with a split personality to be a real saint of God.

Except for children born schizophrenic, I do not believe that Satan can get a firm hold upon a person, to the extent of schizophrenia, unless he is permitted to do so. The Bible tells us to resist the devil and he will flee. (James

4:7.) This means that from our youth we should try to be like Jesus in all our actions and to resist the devil in all areas of our lives. In so doing, we discover the secret to a normal mental life.

Some schizophrenics were born mentally maladjusted. Sometimes, especially in the heathen world, certain people are born possessed of the devil. Arlindo, the witch doctor from Brazil, was baptized to the devil in a voodoo worship before he was born. A witch doctor poured warm chicken blood over his mother in the form of a cross and dedicated him to the devil. At the age of three, he engaged in the mystic writing of prescriptions for those who were sick.

There are strange abnormalities, physical and mental, which can come at birth. However, most often a broken personality is the result of decisions which were made by the individual involved.

I would not say that a person considered to have a split personality must necessarily be demon possessed. It might be that he is only oppressed of the devil. Acts 10:38 says: *God anointed Jesus of Nazareth with the Holy Ghost and with power: who went about doing good, and healing all that were oppressed of the devil; for God was with him.*

In a case of schizophrenia, the minister would need to possess divine authority to rebuke the sickness for the sick person to be set free.

I know from many experiences that Christ can heal a mental illness as simply as He can heal a physical illness. He designed and created the entire human personality, so no human need is beyond His healing and helping hand.

So, have faith in God. Bring every need to the Master Physician.

39. Can a Christian become demon possessed?

In my seminars in the cities of America I am probably asked this question more often than any other. I do not understand why this matter should be a problem to the Christian Church.

The Bible says plainly in James 4:7, *Submit yourselves therefore to God. Resist the devil, and he will flee from you.* There are two aspects of this verse. First, to submit ourselves to God means that we are never to submit to the devil's presence or his deceiving ways. Secondly, we are told to resist the devil. To resist is an action that shows strength. God declares through the Bible that upon this action the devil will flee from us. To flee is not just to crawl or to walk or even to run. A fleeing person runs away in terror.

When the devil understands that a Christian has a strong hold on God and is resisting him, the Bible declares that he **will** flee. I have found the Bible to be true.

One cannot imagine Simon Peter or the Apostle Paul being afraid of demon possession. Yet throughout the world I have been asked literally hundreds of times: "Can a Christian be possessed?"

I feel the correct way to answer this question is to first state the Christian's position in Christ. When Christ sent out

His twelve apostles, He gave them power and authority over devils. Matthew 10:1 states: *And when he had called unto him his twelve disciples, he gave them power against unclean spirits, to cast them out, and to heal all manner of sickness and all manner of disease.*

Jesus did not tell His disciples to protect themselves against demon power. Above all, He did not warn them that they might become possessed or injured while rebuking demons. He gave them divine authority over all demonic forces.

Later the Lord sent forth His seventy disciples, which would be His second line of offense. These men were not of the same caliber as the first twelve, but they were apostles since the word *apostle* means "a sent one." Again, Jesus gave these men explicit power not only to heal the sick, but also to cast out devils:

And the seventy returned again with joy, saying, Lord, even the devils are subject unto us through thy name.

And he said unto them, I beheld Satan as lightning fall from heaven. Behold, I give unto you power to tread on serpents and scorpions, and over all the power of the enemy: and nothing shall by any means hurt you.

Luke 10:17-19

Christ did not tell the seventy in any way to protect themselves against demon power or to be careful in the way they handled evil spirits. He did not warn them of any personal danger. He commanded them to cast out devils without fear or favor, assuring them that "nothing shall by any means hurt you."

One of the amazing and challenging articles in the Great Commission, which happens to be the final words ever spoken on the face of this earth by the Lord Jesus Christ during His ministry, was when He assured His disciples, *And these signs shall follow them that believe; In my name shall they cast out devils* (Mark 16:17).

Here again, in His final commission before going back to sit at the right hand of the Father in heaven, Christ's last instructions were to deliver people who are possessed of devils. He did not imply in any way that these devils could hurt believers or could even stand up against them. The disciples were told to cast them out!

The Word of God says further: *Submit yourselves therefore to God. Resist the devil, and he will flee from you* (James 4:7).

The Word of God is either true or not true. If we as Christians have authority to resist the devil, we must obey. The word *resist* is a military word. It indicates offensive action. It means to take the initiative.

If Christians actively, persistently, dogmatically, and spiritually resist the devil, then the Bible says he will flee. If the devil will run from us in terror, why should Christians be afraid of him? How can he hurt us? This is the positive side of Christian security and power.

On the other hand, when the Lord Jesus cast out a deaf spirit, He called it a spirit of deafness. (Mark 9:25.) He also cast out dumbness, calling it a spirit of dumbness. (Matt. 9:32,33.)

Now no person would for a moment say that all the deaf and dumb people in the world will go to hell. Yet the Bible says that it is a spirit which has made some of them deaf and dumb.

A person can be a devoted Christian and love God, yet be totally deaf or dumb. According to the ministry of Jesus Christ, this means that some forms of deafness or dumbness are caused by the devil.

How is it possible for a professing Christian to become demon possessed? A woman definitely under the power of the devil was asked, "Evil spirit, how did you get into this woman?" The spirit answered back, "At the movie theater. I was there and had a right to go into her."

This opened up a tremendous avenue of thinking for me. I began to realize that if a Christian is out of bounds and in the wrong place, he does not bear divine protection. If Jesus were on this earth, He would not frequent filthy, immoral theaters to be contaminated by sensual suggestions and obscenities.

So, when you go into the devil's territory, it is possible to become a victim of whatever he offers, even though you claim to be a Christian at the time.

When we lived in Hong Kong, we had the full protection of American might and of British strength as long as we stayed on the right side of the border. I looked across the border many times, but I never wanted to go into Communist China. If I had crossed that border, my protective rights would have ceased. The same is true of Christian living.

I am personally convinced that anger can be a spirit and can actually make a person insane. In Denver, Colorado, I was asked to pray for a man in a nursing home who was paralyzed. I was told that his condition was the result of a fit of anger.

While I was praying for a motion picture actor in Manila who had suffered two strokes, his wife told me that both strokes came upon him during a violent rage.

I am also convinced that adultery is a spirit. Multitudes of people testify that the demonic urge to commit adultery overwhelms them. One man told me that cold perspiration dropped from his fingers and he trembled all over until he stopped resisting and submitted to the evil spirit, yet he was a prominent church worker.

This means a professing Christian can open the door of his soul and spirit to lust, jealousy, or lying. Paul said in 2 Timothy 2:24-26:

And the servant of the Lord must not strive; but be gentle unto all men, apt to teach, patient, in meekness instructing those that oppose themselves; if God peradventure will give them repentance to the acknowledging of the truth; and that they may recover themselves out of the snare of the devil, who are taken captive by him at his will.

Then can a Christian become demon possessed? For many years I would have said unequivocally no, but through the experience of meeting so many people who claim to be Christians and seeing them under the power of the devil, I had to come up with some answers.

People who claim to know God but who live a fleshly carnal life open the door of their spirit and soul to the devil. He takes advantage of them and dominates them through evil desires. They find themselves in the clutches of Satan and can only be set free by the power of God.

God's Word says, . . . *be filled with the Spirit* (Eph. 5:18). In so doing, you give no place to the devil. Those who do not follow this command to be filled with the Spirit give place to the devil to enter their lives.

40. Is deliverance of a city the same as a personal deliverance?

My wife labored in Argentina for about eight years. She can tell you that it was one of the hardest places in the world to preach. Many people preached there for years with almost no results.

Then a Bible school group began to fast and pray. As they fasted and prayed, they felt a great deliverance.

Evidently they had an experience in this prayer meeting of casting down a power—almost like the one I had in Manila—but with a city rather than a person. When they cast down that power, tremendous revival came to the Argentine. It was so mighty that I understand a million people were saved in one revival meeting. The battle of the world is spiritual. You have to believe that.

41. If you saw a "mad dog" which was injuring people, would you lay hands on it?

If it were my animal and I wanted to preserve its life, I would pray for it. If it were not mine, I would let the city or the owner take care of it. I've known of many people who have prayed for animals and God has done a miracle for them. But I think God normally does His miracles for humans.

42. What is the best way to close down pornographic movie theaters?

The best way is to find out who the officials of the city are who give out licenses to such places and talk with them in a group large enough to get their attention. Tell them that if they want to stay in office, they should not license such businesses.

We are the government, and the people we put into office must be made aware of our desires and beliefs. We should let those in office know that as citizens we will not tolerate such things in our community. That's the best way to stop it, by legal means. Don't take the law into your own hands. That's not right.

43. When a member of your family is in a rage, should you come against the spirit at that moment or later?

I think I would do it later, because the intimacy there is so strong that you will only have a battle in the house. If you wait until later and say, ''Now that thing that was manifesting itself wasn't really you. You're too nice to act like that," that person will usually respond, "Yes, that's right." Then you can tell him, "Jesus will set you free from that, if you will let Him." When he agrees, you can just do it and it's finished. However, you must realize that even God cannot set a person free unless he wants to be free.

44. **Angels can appear visibly in bodily form as Gabriel appeared to Mary. Can demons, as fallen angels, have bodies of their own? Can they come to a person on their own, or do they need a human or an animal host?**

I don't really know if demons appear bodily as did the angels who came to eat with Abraham. Long Giveratnum, a famous Indian minister, told me that once he was going to a certain place to preach. As he was walking along, he met a very beautiful Indian girl who tried to seduce him. He said that he just closed his eyes and said, "Oh, the blood of Jesus." When he opened his eyes, no one could be found. He searched and yelled, but he couldn't find anybody. He was sure that the girl was a demon and that if he had accepted the seduction he would have lost his anointing. He would have been having fornication with a demon.

That is what he said, but I don't know about such as this. I'm going to be honest with you and admit that's where we can learn together.

45. Are inhibitions an indication of oppression?

Yes. Inhibitions are the holding back and holding down of the human personality. God made us to express ourselves freely and openly, to speak forth and to let our natures flow forth without obstruction. The only way a spiritual person can bless others is by flowing. God doesn't want us inhibited. He wants us set free by His mighty power. Don't let anything inhibit you, in Jesus' name.

46. If a member of the family not living at home has regressed and is repressed, may he be set free simply by ministering the prayer of deliverance?

If you've left home and you're depressed, forget home and get your deliverance. Talk to the devil and say, "I will not accept your darkness, your clouds, your sorrows. I will not accept them, and I will not accept a downcast spirit because God lifts me up. I am a son of God. I am a prince with God and I will rejoice in my Maker. I will win souls, and you'd better get out of the way!" You will not have depression at that point.

47. Can people who are in the first five stages of possession be set free? Is the procedure the same?

Yes, it is exactly the same. But people can also set themselves free in the first stages of demon possession or oppression. When you realize that you are sad or depressed all the time, recognize that it is the devil who is doing it to you. You can just rebel against sadness by saying, "I'm going to have joy. I'm going to have it right now, and I thank God for it." Then start laughing and claim the joy!

48. **Can a born-again, Spirit-filled Christian work in bars and clubs serving drinks? Isn't it Satan who creeps in and deceives such people into thinking that it is all right to do so, that they can witness for Jesus while serving drinks?**

I think you have the answer right there. Dear Christian, never let the devil fool you in this way. When you're on his territory, he's the captain. You had better get back where Jesus is the Captain. Don't play around with the devil. Anytime you go to a negative place, thinking you're going to do good there, the devil has deceived you.

Hundreds of people have said to me, "I know that church over there is dead. I'm going to go and revive them." They're wrong! They are not going to revive that church; they are just going to dig a hole for themselves. I can tell you right now that until the pastor gets revived, no church will ever be revived, because God cannot go one step further than the pastor.

49. In casting out devils I have heard you exclaim, "Come out!" Do you ever bind Satan or mention his name? When I have cast out devils, some people have taken offense because they thought I had called them Satan or a devil.

You got into trouble, didn't you? I don't think there have ever been two cases that we have dealt with which were exactly alike. I don't believe there were ever two cases that Jesus dealt with in just the same way. He didn't heal people the same way every time. We deal with different conditions in different ways.

Normally when you come against Satan, you identify him. Then you give your reasons for exorcising authority over him: "By the blood of Jesus Christ I come (because it is all-powerful), and I come by the authority of the Great Commission."

Normally that's the way it is done. If you do it another way and it works, then the Lord knows your heart. It is not the words we use that are important; it is the spirit in which we act. You may have a drive inside you that motivates you to action. You can't say very much; you just scream, "Come out!" But the demons obey, and the person is set free.

50. In commanding a spirit to come out, can you direct it to go forth to one place or another?

If you can bring a spirit out, you can direct it, at least locally. You can tell it to go to some uninhabited place or into the uninhabited space above us. Retaining the spirit there is something else. I don't think you can bind spirits in that way, but you can tell them to go. If you have the power to bring them out, no doubt they will obey you in this second stage.

51. Please explain binding of the devil. Is it permanent or temporary?

Binding the devil has to be temporary, because he and his demons will not be permanently bound until the end of the Great Tribulation. The demons who were bound in Jesus' day are the same demons who are working in the world today.

52. How can you help a person stay free when you cannot be with him; for example, a person in a mental hospital?

I would think that in the first moment of the release of pressure you would bring him out of that place. He needs to be away from the negative influence inside that institution. It's bad. There's no faith there.

Then he will need to have the Word of God read to him, to be in real spiritual services, to be taught to sing choruses and to pray—almost as you would teach a baby—to bring him into spiritual depth and blessing. If he doesn't walk in that fullness, he won't have any means of remaining free.

Above all, start quoting him the promises of God. Sustain him with that strength.

53. Please expound on the dangers of modern music and dance prevalent in our society today and their relationship to satanic bondage.

I read just the other day where some film makers were shooting a film in Africa. They had just started playing the music for the film when one of the tribal people came to them and said, ''I wouldn't play that music if I were you.''

''Why not?'' asked the film crew.

''Well,'' responded the tribesman, ''I don't know where you got it, but that is the music we use to call up the dead spirits to worship them.''

The modern world has gone to the pagan, heathen peoples and brought back the offbeat and hard beat rhythms they use. Without knowing it, many of our young people today are worshiping the devil.

When I was in Brazil, one third of all the people were spiritists. I never had to cast out so many devils anywhere in the world as I did in Brazil. Every third person in any gathering was a spiritist. While I was there, they told me that American musicians and dancers came from places like New York and Chicago to record their music and take it back to teach Americans.

If you pick up the devil's music and start singing it and playing it, you're involving yourself with hell. I would say that any kind of music which tears up a person's insides the way rock music does destroys spiritual strength and power. Young people who constantly play it at an ear-splitting level until it pounds into their brains show that they are already very close to possession.

Any time a person abandons his mind like this and throws it into neutral, so to speak, he opens his spirit to demonic possession. You should never do that. Keep your mind strong and alert and controlled—keep it on Jesus.

54. **Please comment on the addiction to television and other diversions that would be a distraction to the Christian walk.**

In Germany and in England recently a certain society gave about 300 families in each of these countries a certain amount of money every week for a period of thirteen weeks if they would allow their TV sets to be sealed up. They were actually paid **not** to watch television. Then these people were monitored by psychologists and sociologists to determine the effects of TV withdrawal upon them.

In a very short while, many of these people went into some sort of delirium tremens. Finally not one single family could stand it. They became so nervous and neurotic that they actually began to shake. They were like drug addicts. They had to have their daily "fix" of television.

Probably ninety-five percent of what is on television is bad. There is always a love scene in every show and usually it is a dirty love scene. How could you have faith in doctors after seeing how they are depicted on the tube with every doctor playing around with somebody else's wife?

Television has no relationship with reality at all. It is just one big lie. If a person is going to drink in all that junk, it will have an effect upon him. There is no way around it. The only answer for a

Christian is to turn off that type program and not allow it into his house. We must guard our minds and spirits and those of our children against the devastating effects of TV's distorted portrayal of life.

55. Where did Jesus direct the demonic spirits to go? I would want to send them to the right place.

First of all, don't misdirect them. For example, if you should say to a spirit, ''Go back to hell from whence you came,'' he won't even come out, because he hasn't gone to hell yet and he's still active. He's one of the fallen spirits that fell from heaven with Satan and until Satan is incarcerated, they're not incarcerated either. At the end of the age, they will be bound there forever with Satan, but not until then. They're not in hell. If you tell them to go back to hell, they will know that you don't understand what you're doing and they won't obey you at all.

One time the Lord Jesus permitted some spirits to go into a herd of pigs.

That was the only time we know of that He allowed such a thing.

I don't know if it's really important to tell them where to go. I just command them to come out. If I do send them somewhere, I will say, "Go into the void of space, into the emptiness of space." That's out of the way of human beings.

You might ask, "Do they obey you?"

That I don't know. There is no way for me to check to see if they really go there or not.

Sometimes I order them: "You go into the uninhabited places of the earth." Maybe you don't realize it, but evil spirits dwell in forests and other places like that. People who know about these things can tell you that there are things out there that you'd never dream. So it is good to send evil spirits away from inhabited places. Since you are not their boss, the devil might send them right back from these places, and they'll obey him. When you tell them to come forth from a person, they must do so. That is about the extent of your jurisdiction over them.

56. There are many books in print about deliverance. How do we know which of these books are harmful and which are beneficial to the student of the Word?

The Bible is the best book for problem solving, including the casting out of devils. I want to see how Jesus did it. If He took one hour or one minute to deliver a person, I want to do it the way He did it.

Before you read a book on deliverance, check on the inside cover to see who published it. The name of the publishing house will tell you if it was published by evangelicals or by a cult. This can be a clue to you whether or not it is okay.

57. When a person has been delivered, does he have to get into the Word and stay in the Word to remain free or healed? For example, if someone comes from a denomination that does not preach the full Gospel, but practices a ritualistic form of worship, what then?

When Paul was saved, he left the First Church of the Pharisees and joined the First Church of the Pentecostals, and it did not offend him to do so. A person should not attend a church because his grandmother went there or because his friends go there. He should choose a church because he receives spiritual food there. He should find a church where the Spirit of the Lord is; otherwise, he will eventually die spiritually for lack of nourishment.

58. When casting out devils, what is the evidence that a person has been delivered?

Joy! His eyes clear up, and his body becomes supple. Many times you can feel the demons moving in the area of the belly. When they are gone, the stomach of the delivered one is soft. Sometimes there are manifestations such as vomiting, but we discourage that. We tell the spirit not to vomit when he gets out—just to get out! We do not encourage manifestations of any kind; in fact, we limit them. Because he is a spirit, he can go out from any part of the body such as the mouth or any other part. He has met his master and he has to go!

59. Is it possible that some congregations have been taught an experience of speaking in tongues, but instead of receiving God's power, they receive a satanic power with their tongues? For example, I heard of a person who visited a church where the people appeared to be praying in tongues, and the piano started playing by itself.

In all my travels in over 100 countries of the world, I have never had anything like that happen, so I tend to doubt it. When there is anything as important as a move of God, there needs to be a spiritual leader who can direct the congregation. I find that problems always arise when we do not have proper leadership. Had I been in the above-mentioned church, I would have cast the devil out of the piano. The devil would like to make counterfeits, but you just keep throwing him out.

60. Was Jesus able to cast out devils by just coming into the presence of demon-possessed people, or did He have to speak to the demons and command them to come out?

Jesus did everything that He did just as we do it. Jesus performed His miracles as the Son of Man. There would not have been miracles if He had acted as God, because God does not know what a miracle is since He is the Creator of all the universe. There were people who passed right by Jesus who did not receive anything, but those who called upon Him were the ones who received deliverance and were set free.

Jesus did not perform miracles because He was the Son of God, but because He was full of the Holy Ghost. We have the same Holy Ghost in us and that is the reason we can set people free.

61. I have a son in Las Vegas who is possessed. Can a spirit in him be cast out by someone who lives several hundred miles away?

Distance is not important in setting a person free. However, your son must want to be set free since God will not overrule our spirits. We are free moral agents. If a person is crazy (totally out of his mind), you can cast the devil out of him, then ask him if he wants to live for Jesus. If he doesn't, the demons will return, even bringing with them more of their kind. (Matt. 12:43-45.)

62. A friend confesses that her dead mother visits her and talks with her. What kind of spirit is this, and should we cast it out?

It is a familiar spirit that seeks to imitate another person. These spirits can do so in a very unusual way, even taking on that person's speech and mannerisms. But you must not believe a familiar spirit. This woman needs to be set free.

63. My sister and her husband bought a house six months ago which had been used as a house of prostitution. Since they took over this house, my aunt has observed a growing anger and bitterness on the part of the husband toward his

wife. They are remodeling the house and have not yet moved in. How do I pray for them and the house?

I heard of a man in England who moved into a house where there were demons. Two of his three daughters died in the same bedroom before he had sense enough to move out. When they investigated the history of that house, they found that a great tragedy had occurred in that room many years before. Obviously it was still demon infested.

When evil spirits dwell in a house, there are two things that can be done:

1. You can go from room to room and cleanse it by pleading the blood of Jesus and commanding the evil spirits to go. You encircle the entire house with the blood of Jesus. Then tell the people who live there to shout the praises of God. If the least manifestation occurs, they should scream, ''Don't you come back! You stay gone forever!'' They will be free.

2. The alternative is for the inhabitants to move out of the house. There are people who are weak in the Spirit and who cannot wage the spiritual warfare necessary.

You can pray the demon out or get out yourself. Personally, I would rather have the devil move!

64. **I have a business acquaintance whose wife has been unusually ill for the last two years. While talking to her, I found that she had had her fortune told when she was a little girl. She was told that she would die this year. Also, her mother had been told when she would die, and she died the appointed year. What can be done?**

Plead the blood of Jesus over her and send the curse back where it came from. Of course, she has to receive it and believe it.

When someone wants to put a curse on me, I command the curse to go back to them doubly. I tell them that I don't believe in curses; but since they do, they can take a double dose. It really scares them. Balaam said, *How shall I curse, whom God hath not cursed?* (Num. 23:8).

65. **I have two Christian friends who are plagued by evil spirits. One has been a Christian for fourteen months, but believes that her husband and children would be better off if she took her own life. The other one, whose husband is studying for the ministry, has times of severe depression which make her sick. What should be done in such cases?**

The devil would like to destroy all of us, and he tries to tell us to take our own lives. In a case like this, we just do not listen to the devil.

When we feel unwanted and unloved, we must ask ourselves: To whom have I shown love lately? If you want to be loved, start loving someone else. Be generous, and you will find that love begets love.

66. What is the difference between oppression and possession?

Possession is the complete take-over of a personality. To oppress means to press down. There is a world of difference between the two. When you are **oppressed,** you can say, "Go," and the oppression has to go. But you cannot deliver yourself from demon **possession.** You must have someone to help you because you are a prisoner at that time.

67. When you are delivering someone, how important is it to know what evil spirit you are dealing with?

It is not necessary to know what spirit is possessing a person to deliver him. Many times it is obvious what kind of spirit it is, such as a deaf spirit. If you don't know, just command the evil spirit to go, and it will go regardless of what kind it is.

68. In the story in Matthew 8:28-34, why did the demons want to go into the herd of pigs, and why did Jesus allow them to do so?

Demons must have a body in order to manifest themselves and to do the things they wish to do. They will reside in humans or animals, wherever they can gain entrance.

69. Can a demon-possessed person resist Satan, or does he have to do what he is told by him?

The demon-possessed girl in the Bilibid Prison in Manila, Philippines, told me that the devil wanted her to go away with him, but she refused to go. Even though she was possessed, she had her own right of will. The possessed boy who kept disappearing told me the same thing. There were things the spirit wanted him to do that he refused to do.

I believe this is very significant. Even when the devil possesses a person, that person's will is still there.

70. Our son belongs to a club in high school that originated from a current popular game based on the Middle Ages. We understand that some of the teachers, as well as

students, play this game. Is this a spiritually dangerous game?

There are many good games available; but some games being introduced today as challenging games of skill and intellect are actually promoting elements of sorcery, witchcraft, and divination. The players are persuaded to develop their imaginations to explore evil characteristics and the casting of actual spells. This indeed is dangerous and can open up an avenue for demonic oppression and influence over the player's life.

71. Can a person who is always tired be oppressed by a spirit of weariness?

Yes. I knew a man who was totally exhausted every time I saw him. He could stay in bed for two or three days and still be tired. It was not a fatal sickness to him, but his wife died caring for him. Constant weariness is of Satan and needs to be rebuked. I command strength to come to me daily.

72. Is gluttony a spirit?

Gluttony **can** be a spirit. When someone has an abnormal desire for food, that desire is a spirit. We should not be under bondage to anything, such as smoking, overeating, or any other harmful habit. Take authority over such things and command them to get out of your life. We are not slaves; we are free in Christ!

73. Why are playing cards a symbol of the devil's power?

If you would study the history of cards, you would find that for hundreds of years they have been associated with immorality. They have traditionally been dedicated to that which is evil. It is not the paper itself that is evil, but that with which cards have been associated.

74. Does a Halloween jack-o'-lantern have any connection with demon power?

The Halloween celebrations should be avoided. Witches and such things are from the devil, and we should never join the devil in any of his celebrations.

75. Is the cross with a loop at the top a symbol of Satan? I have heard that it is used in Satan worship and is connected with Egyptian religions.

I would not want to be associated with anything connected with the ancient Egyptian religions. If a person wants to wear a cross, it should be something simple.

76. Is it right to have religious symbols and pictures of Jesus hanging in one's home? Isn't this idol worship?

God has symbols, and it is not offensive to me to have a picture of Jesus hanging in the room.

It is dangerous, however, when people make that picture a symbol of power and attribute strength to it. Satan will use such things as a symbol of his presence if he can.

God wants to be worshiped in spirit and in truth, so we need to be careful. As a piece of art, however, such objects are perfectly all right.

77. Are fetishes and emblems used in jewelry considered emblems of demon power?

Yes. I wouldn't have one around whether it is made in this country or elsewhere. Have no relationship with anything connected with demon power.

78. Can people who are heavily sedated because they are possessed be set free?

We have seen several people who were drunk be totally set free and made sober. If they then wish to love and serve God, they will remain free.

79. If sickness is demon related, what causes it?

A person can be sick because of overeating or from eating the wrong things. Sickness can also be caused from overwork or deterioration of various organs in the body. Worry, stress, jealousy, etc., can cause sickness and disease.

There are many reasons for illness that have nothing to do with demons.

In these cases, one can pray for healing or contact a doctor. Sometimes a person can be attacked by Satan, as was the case with Job, and can be set free by God's mighty power.

80. Are there examples of inner healing in the Bible?

One example is the woman who was caught in the act of adultery. (John 8:3-11.) Jesus said to her, "Where are your accusers?" She replied, "I don't have any." He then told her, "Neither do I condemn you. Go and sin no more." This would be an inner healing —to go from the bottom of corruption to a level of purity and holiness.

81. Are wars and killings from the devil? Do you feel it is right for a Christian to protect our country?

If America is in trouble, we can either fight for our liberty, or we can lie down and allow some other country to become our master. Personally, I would rather die fighting for my liberty than die in jail.

82. You mentioned that you have felt movements in the abdominal area of a person being delivered. Is this phenomena found only in a person who is possessed?

Evil spirits can move around in various parts of the body. Satan mainly seeks to take over in two areas: the throne of the soul, which is the head, and the throne of the spirit, which is the belly. Some who are possessed complain of feeling bands around their head; but when the power of Satan is broken, the bands are gone.

83. Can a person deliver himself from possession or oppression?

There are several steps to total possession. In the cases of repression, depression, or oppression, a person can deliver himself. He can say, "I demand oppression to go from me and I am free!" However, when it becomes obsession, his mind is afflicted and he cannot set himself free. Someone else must do it for him because he cannot even think clearly and does not have faith or strength.

84. **In 1 Samuel 28:3-20 when King Saul went to the witch of Endor and asked her to call up Samuel from the dead, was it Samuel that the witch brought up or a demon?**

This was a very unusual situation where the whole nation was in great trouble. Yes, it was Samuel who came up. He rebuked Saul and told him that his kingdom was gone. It was the dividing of a kingdom and the end of a dynasty. Only in similar circumstances where there was something of this importance to the Kingdom of God would this sort of thing be repeated.

85. **Does inner healing have anything to do with deliverance?**

Yes, it has to do with deliverance. For instance, if a person is sad or depressed continually, he needs to be delivered by God's power. That is inner healing.

86. **A friend has been seeing what she believes to be angels. I told her to test the spirits, but she insists that they make her feel peaceful. Is**

there anything I could tell her to do to see if these are angels or demons?

They are not angels of light. Angels are messengers of God. They deliver their message and leave. This type of spirit is what we call a "familiar spirit." It will take greater advantage of her all the time until she is unable to sleep at night.

87. When a woman receives an obscene phone call, should she hang up or rebuke the devil?

When a woman gets such a call, she should say, "Devil, come out of him!" in a strong voice and hang up. That person will not call back.

88. Explain Matthew 7:22,23 in which Jesus said: *Many will say to me in that day, Lord, Lord, have we not prophesied in thy name? and in thy name have cast out devils? and in thy name done many wonderful works? And then will I profess unto them, I never knew you: depart from me, ye that work iniquity.*

We are sons of God by the blood of Jesus. In the Judgment, people such as witch doctors and Christian Scientists will say, "Haven't we healed in Your name?" But Jesus will say to them, "I never knew you." This is because they have never been in the family of God. They are not backsliders; they simply have never been born again by the blood of Jesus.

89. **I have a collection of Beatle records. Is it all right to sell them and give the money to the Lord's work, or should I destroy them?**

Destroy them! They might send someone to hell. The beat in such music is the beat of the jungle, and it will tear apart a person's insides.

90. **Do you consider such things as magic tricks, sleight of hand, ventriloquism, Halloween masks, etc., to be evil?**

We have a whole lesson available on the symbolisms of demon power. Don't play with things connected with demon power; leave them alone.

91. What is an enchanter?

An enchanter is one who hypnotizes; he enchants people. They say that a serpent looking at a bird enchants it. He moves closer and closer to the bird while staring into the bird's eyes until he captures it.

92. A lady heard her dead husband calling her name as she was waking up one morning. Would that be a familiar spirit who spoke to her?

No, it would be a deceiving spirit since it was not her husband calling. If that happens to you, don't keep listening to that kind of spirit. It will torment you if you listen to it.

93. Please explain what is wrong about the writings of Kahlil Gibran? A friend reads them and sees nothing wrong with them, but I feel that they are not right.

This work is spiritism of the highest form, and God does not want us to be associated with it in any way. It can get into your spirit.

94. Who created sin and evil?

Sin is transgression, and transgression is rebellion. Sin was born in the heart of an archangel named Lucifer. He caused rebellion in heaven and was cast out. Then he brought it to earth where he planted it in the hearts of Adam and Eve. They in turn rebelled against God. Rebellion is sin, and all sin is evil. Through Adam, sin entered the bloodstream of humanity. The only way a human can get rid of that sin is by the blood of Jesus. There is no other way.

95. Since everything in heaven is pure and good, how could Lucifer live there and become proud and start all the evil which is in the world?

Evil does not begin on the outside; it begins in the heart. Lucifer looked in the mirror and said, "You are the most beautiful one here. You should be above everything else, including God." He should have resisted those thoughts, but instead he conceived them, brought them to birth, and acted upon them. Evil can come in the sweetest of places if it is allowed to generate inside a person.

96. Why did Lucifer not have the knowledge to know that he did not have the power to overthrow the throne of God?

When a person becomes conceited and full of himself, he does not see clearly. If you talk to prisoners in a jail, most of them will say, ''I have been wronged. I am not guilty. I shouldn't be here.'' They will invariably blame all their misfortunes on others.

97. Can a Christian deliver someone else when he has sin in his own life?

Study the life of Samson. He had the power of God in his life even when he lived in sin. When a person receives a spiritual gift from God, it will work in his life until he breaks his covenant with God. Samson's covenant with God was that he would not cut his hair nor drink wine nor touch the dead. He did things that were wrong and seemed to escape the consequences. They eventually brought him to the point where he broke his covenant with God. When that happened, he became as any other man; his eyes were gouged out and he died among the enemies of God.

98. James 4:7 says, *Submit yourselves therefore to God. Resist the devil, and he will flee from you.* **How can we submit ourselves to God?**

Submitting ourselves to God can have to do with our businesses, our domestic lives, and our own spiritual lives. To submit to God means to give oneself fully on a daily basis to the Lord in all these areas. We should submit ourselves to the Word of God and do what it says.

99. A relative of mine says that he believes in God, but he is a Hindu. Is Hinduism devil worship?

Hindu gods are spirits. If your relative is attached to a Hindu deity, and most likely he is, that deity is an evil spirit. If he is worshiping that deity and if he has a *mantra* (a secret word that he receives from a guru and which he keeps repeating inside), that is an open door for the devil. By putting his mind in neutral, which is what the *mantra* accomplishes, evil spirits can enter in through the unguarded door to his mind.

In a way, all heathen are under the oppression of the devil because they have believed a lie. They have over 300 million gods, so everything is a god, and that is not truth. There is only one God, and that one God has one Son, the Lord Jesus. There is one Holy Spirit Who comes forth from the Father and the Son to bless us and walk with us.

100. How can a lying spirit and a lust-ful spirit be cast out of a family? One man I know is the father of six children, but cannot stay home.

God will not make anyone live right. For instance, He did not make Adolph Hitler live right. We are free moral agents who can choose to go to heaven or to hell. If this man does not want to serve God, he won't serve and love Him, and he won't love his family. All you can do is pray that the devil's power will be broken from his life. He must want to be free from the spirits that bind him before he can be free. He cannot be free by your wanting him to be free.

101. Is there a spirit of gambling?

Gambling is an attempt to get something for nothing, and that is wrong. The gambling casinos of Las Vegas and Atlantic City are programmed to take people's money. They will allow them to win some money just to keep them interested, but in the end they will lose. Those who have a gambling spirit would steal the booties off their babies to get money to gamble. They need to be set free by the mighty power of God.

For additional copies of
101 Questions and Answers On Demon Powers,
write:

HARRISON HOUSE
P. O. Box 35035 • Tulsa, OK 74153